DORDOGNE ON A BUDGET

PATRICK DELAFORCE

rosters

Published by ROSTERS LTD.
23 Welbeck Street, London W1
© Rosters Ltd.
ISBN 0-948032-83-9

First Edition 1990

Designed and published by ROSTERS
Typeset by JH Graphics Ltd, Reading, Berkshire.
Printed and bound in Great Britain by Cox & Wyman Ltd,
Reading, Berkshire.

CONTENTS

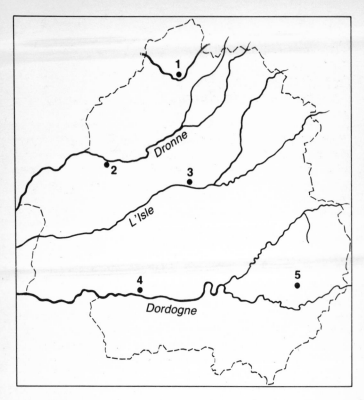

1 Nontron
2 Riberac
3 Périgueux
4 Bergerac
5 Sarlat

Part One:
Discovering Dordogne

CHAPTER ONE:
LAND OF DREAMS

"France may one day exist no more, but the Dordogne will live on just as dreams live on and nourish the souls of men." So wrote Henry Miller about one of the most scenic regions of France and incidentally an area where you can nourish the body with a cuisine second to none. To help the dreams along why not try a glass of local wine − the secret red Pécharmant for example is worthy of a trip on its own account.

In this book I have tried to share my love of Dordogne, its people, food and wine. For 25 years my wife and I have visited the region. We used to own a country farm in neighbouring Lot and our cousins lived in a beautifully restored manor house perched on the Lot/Dordogne border. It is not hard to see why the region is already a firm favourite with the British, especially those looking for a home away from home. Some 5,000 Britons have opted for a piece of the French countryside where they can enjoy a marvellous climate and scenery which at its best simply takes your breath away. The summers are warm and balmy, spring and autumn are enchanting and the winter is short and mild. There are wide rivers swathing valleys, castles atop little hills and diminutive villages where you may well spot locals sporting black berets and playing boules in the main square in the shade of the giant plane trees.

For the gourmet the region is one delicious dish after another. In Chapter Five I have described some of my favourite recipes − but even those of you who choose a picnic will find a marvellous array of delicacies on the stalls of the local markets. You can discover unusual varieties of cheese, honeycombs, walnuts, fruits and vegetables of all kinds. Wine buffs such as myself can savour the fine wines of Bergerac and Monbazillac, as well as a range of regional wines. More about that in Chapter Twelve.

The natives are friendly — but few speak English. Despite the fact that the region was ruled from London for three centuries in the Middle Ages and that the Brits have arrived in force the locals stick doggedly to French. In Chapter Seventeen I give you some basic phrases to ease your way — but don't forget the universal gestures of the pointed finger, the shoulder shrug and most important of all — the smile.

Discovering Dordogne

Known to the French as **Périgord**, the Dordogne is the third largest department in France with a land mass of 9,224 square kilometres and a population of about 400.000. A quarter of the region is still forest, and pollution mercifully is minimal, except in mid-summer. **Limoges** lies a hundred kilometres to the north, **Bordeaux** 120 kilometres to the southwest and **Cahors** 140 kilometres to the southeast.

Michelin maps 72 and 75 cover the area. In this book I have concentrated not only on the actual department of the Dordogne but also on the area to the east where the river Dordogne flows through the Lot department which is known as *Quercy* to the French.

The Dordogne is surrounded by seven other departments. To the north the Charente and Haute Vienne, to the west Charente Maritime and the Gironde, to the south the Lot et Garonne and the Lot and finally to the east, the Corrèze. The Dordogne itself is oval shaped with Périgueux in the centre, and has a radius of 60-70 kilometres.

Historically the Dordogne is divided into four colourful regions. The northern section, which includes Nontron, Brantôme, Riberac, Thiviers and Lanouaille, is known as 'Périgord vert' since it is so verdantly wooded. The chalky central region west and east of the large prefecture town of Périgueux is known as 'Périgord blanc'. This mainly farming area includes Montpon-Menestrol and Mussidan in the west and Savignac and Hautfort in the east. The southwest around Bergerac is known as 'Périgord pourpre' on account of its purple wines. Finally the southeastern sector is called 'Périgord noir' and is centred on Sarlat. The dark greeny-black holm-oaks give the region its name of 'noir', and it includes Montignac, Domme, St Cyprien, Belvès and Le Bugue.

Varied pursuits

The area is the richest in France for its prehistory background. The wonderful caves, grottos and abris (shelters) along the river banks of the Vézère, the curious troglodyte rock villages where our ancestors lived and stalked and hunted bison, and the underground cavern of Padirac, rank amongst the natural wonders of the world. Religious sites such as Rocamadour attract pilgrims from around the world to see the black virgin (Madonna) in the chapel of Nôtre Dame. History lovers will visit the bastide towns of Domme, Monpazier and others. Ramblers have a choice of half a dozen well-marked Grande Randonnée trails which criss-cross the region.

For those wet or cold days there are museums, safari parks and sightseeing tours in all the main towns. Chapter Three lists many other activities including horsedrawn caravan holidays, riding centres, fishing and pot-holing. Many towns and villages have swimming pools (piscines) and 'étangs' (man made lakes for bathing and boating).

Although there are many grander châteaux to be found further north along the banks of the river Loire, the Dordogne as a department has more castles and châteaux — nearly 1,200 of them — than any other in France. Most of them are still privately owned, and some indeed are for sale. However, I have listed those which I think should not be missed, including Beynac, Biron, Hautefort and Jumilhac-le-Grand as well as another thirty which in my view merit a detour.

Making your connections

Road, rail and air communications with the Dordogne are excellent. The N21 from Limoges heads south for Périgueux and continues to Bergerac, Villeneuve and Agen. The main road west to east is the N89 from Bordeaux, Libourne to Périgueux, and it continues east to Brive. Main roads feed into the region from Angoulême in the northwest and Cahors from the southeast. I have driven on nearly all the minor roads in the Dordogne. Good surfaces, well signed and rarely used (except in mid-summer), they are an absolute delight. Round each corner lies a 'pigeonnier', a small village with romanesque church, a curious dolmen, a minor château, a friendly, apparently deserted village near a river or a prosperous old farmhouse, surrounded by dappled cows and browsing sheep.

There are railway connections with Paris, Bordeaux and Cahors, and airports served by Air Inter at Périgueux, Bergerac and Domme. It is a pity that you cannot arrive by boat as the Vikings and Normans did a thousand years ago. Five major rivers cross the department — the mighty Dordogne, said to be the second longest in France; its off-shoots the Vézère and Auvézère; the Isle and the Dronne. Not only do these rivers help make for a near perfect climate but also their stately beauty attracts many holidaymakers to sail, kayak or canoe, and swim during the season. A separate chapter lists the many 'campings' to be found in the area. In fact there are more than a hundred different rivers in the region including the Bandiat, Beauronne, Loue, Cern, Chironde, Laurence and Céouck, with altogether 8,000 kilometres (5,000 miles) of river banks.

Ancestral home

I must declare a vested interest in the Dordogne. To the west of Bergerac is the small, undistinguished town of La Force which belonged to my ancestors from about 1000 to 1253 AD. It was part of Eleanor of Aquitaine's dowry when she married Henry Plantagenet in 1152 AD. Two years later he became King Henry II and his two sons grew up in Aquitaine. Our ancestral home was on the fluctuating borders with French-owned France and our luck ran out in 1253. The historic rolls record 'Le Roi d'Angleterre (Henri III) prie le maire et jurats de Bordeaux de l'accompagne en armes juscu'a Bergerac. Le monarque declare que Gaillard (a swashbuckling version of Guillaume-William) de la Force et Helie Prevost ont quitté Bergerac pour rentra son service et qu'il doit réparer les dépenses et les pertes que leur a causé cette demarche.' That same year two of the family went to London as wine shippers from their vineyards near La Réole whilst the rest of the family moved eastwards into the Auvergne. The French Caumont family 'took over' La Force and Henri IV of France promoted Caumont la Force to become a Duchy several centuries later. Oh well, not everybody's dreams can come true in the Dordogne.

CHAPTER TWO:
TRAVELLERS' TIPS

'Dordogne on a Budget' is written for the independent traveller of modest means, travelling by car or caravan, who wishes to enjoy the beautiful countryside, explore the grottos, rivers, châteaux and romanesque churches of the Dordogne — and perhaps give thoughts to buying a second or permanent home. 'The Budget' plan is based on expenditure of approximately 400-450 francs roughly per day per couple. For instance:

		Francs
1.	Double bedroom in modest hotel*	100-120
2.	Continental breakfast for two	35-40
3.	Picnic lunch for two of bread, butter, cheese, fruit and bottle of local wine — from supermarché	40-50
4.	Petrol based on 70-100 km per day	30-40
5.	Château, museum entry charges	30-40
6.	Fixed price dinner for two	100-120
7.	Bottle or pichet of local wine at hotel price	20-30
8.	Coffee, aperitifs or soft drinks	20

*A campsite or 'gite' will be around 60-80 francs.

Don't forget that midday is the clarion call for lunch. Everything stops for two hours while gourmet delights are served and digested. No museum, château or grotto will re-open until 2 p.m. You should make allowance for this strange Gallic habit and either join in with a two hour spread of your own or create a picnic lunch of paté, cheese, fresh fruit, bread and wine.

Travel checklist
Obviously make sure your passport is valid and up to date, your favourite ferry company is not on strike and your tickets

9

are accurate (right days, times and destinations). I recommend not only a green card for your car but also comprehensive insurance for all members of your party. Far better to spend a few more pounds and if anything over-insure your family and all belongings than to penny pinch and suffer the consequences. Selecting cash, credit cards, Eurocheques, travellers cheques or what have you has so many pros and cons. I am a Eurocheque fan, but other people swear by their credit cards. The Michelin maps you need for the Dordogne are Nos. 72 and 75 and can easily be purchased in the UK. Bring some soap too as many modest French hotels are reluctant to provide any.

The choice of route to the Dordogne is usually between the fast auto-routes (all '*péage*' i.e. quite expensive tolls) and the more direct '*route nationale*' or local roads, which are cheaper, usually more interesting but may involve greater map reading skills. Try to arrange any really long drives on a Sunday when the law forbids juggernauts and lesser lorries to travel. Whatever you do, keep away from the Paris '*périphérique*' ring road in the four rush hour periods 8.00 a.m.-9.00 a.m., 11.45 a.m. – 12.15 p.m. (lunch time), 1.45 p.m.-2.15 p.m. (return from lunch) and 6.00 p.m.-7.00 p.m. (office closing times). Also remember the speed limits. These are 130 km/h on autoroutes, 90 km/h on main routes and 60 km/h in towns.

Choice of hotels

There are many good-value one star hotels in France with double rooms available for about 100 francs per night for bed but no meals. There are of course some with indifferent management but in our experience they are all remarkably honest. My wife and I must have stayed in over 300 hotels and never been overcharged. Besides a clean room, comfortable bed, hot water, and the 'noise' factor, in the morning good hot coffee, a warm croissant and fresh bread for breakfast are essential. Also, try to find a hotel with its own private parking. We have suffered at the hands of thieves in several major cities in France, Spain and Portugal. An empty car, well locked and parked under street lighting is the next best thing to a hotel's private car park.

Hotel bookings

Our family tend to make a telephone reservation for the first night of the holiday a few days in advance which gives us some leeway for arrival. Try to arrive before 8.00 p.m. as otherwise the chef will be getting apprehensive in the kitchen if you are any later. Many provincial restaurants serve the evening meal from 7.00 p.m (and lunch from noon).

In France prices are per room irrespective of whether it is for one or two people. Details of prices are displayed in the entrance lobby and hung behind the room door. The receptionist will endeavour to offer you the most expensive room which has not yet been 'sold' for the night. Be firm, look at the room list and ask for a room to suit your budget. Then ask to see it before making a decision. This is normal practice and will not upset the proprietor. Check that the room offered you is not on the noisiest side overlooking a major motorway such as route N21 and preferably not immediately next door to the bathroom.

Although the local police no longer need to examine your passport when you check in at your hotel, you may occasionally be asked to leave it at the desk, theoretically for the gendarmerie. The hotel is in fact taking precautions that you do not slip away early in the morning without paying the bill. Just smile and remember to collect it at breakfast when you pay. Incidentally, all the charges on the bill are net, i.e. 'service compris' − room, breakfast, supper, wine. There is no need to add anything more unless the service has been beyond the call of duty.

If you telephone from the hotel you will be billed a premium charge. Far better to do it from the local PTT or from a *Cabine de Poste*. Cheap rates Monday to Friday 9.30 p.m. to 8.00 a.m., Saturdays after 2.00 p.m., Sundays and public holidays all day. To ring the UK from France from a phonebox feed in, say 10 francs as a credit, dial 19, wait for the tone to change, dial 44, then the STD number (less the first 0), then your number. To phone France from the UK dial 010 33, then the eight figure provincial number. You can receive calls in the box and the number is clearly marked.

Restaurants

Experienced menu-spotters, having arrived at their chosen destination by 6.00 p.m. and parked in the main square often select their hotel by the quality of the dinner promised for that evening. If 'rognons de veau à la périgourdine' is on a menu and the hotel looks reasonable, that place would get my casting vote. Of course, difficulties always arise if you have say four vociferous members of the family with differing tastes. If by any chance the prix fixe menu is **not** handed to you by the waiter, politely but firmly ask for it. The 'plat du jour' is the chef's speciality of the day and should be well-cooked, interesting and inexpensive. As in England the wine list may look too expensive and daunting, so instead ask for a pichet or carafe of 'vin rouge/blanc/rosé de la maison which will appear rapidly at a reasonable price — 20/25 francs per bottle. Try, however, at some stage in your stay to taste a regional wine from Bergerac, Pécharmont or Monbazillac.

Electricity

Electricity is 220 volts, so an adaptor for hairdryer or shaver is necessary with a 2 pin plug. If you are a keen reader and do not fancy French TV in the bar in the evening, take a portable lamp with a 100 watt bulb with you. The hoteliers' thrift often extends from lack of soap to very low powered electric light bulbs!

Illness

If any member of your family has a relatively minor problem the pharmacie with a **green** cross will have a qualified chemist who may be able to suggest treatment. In the event of serious illness he or she will be able to give you the local doctor's address.

French Holidays

These are on January 1st, Easter, May 1st, VE Day on May 8th, Ascension Day, Whitsun weekend, Bastille Day on July 14th, Assumption Day on August 15th, All Saints Day on November 1st, Remembrance Day on November 11th, and Christmas Day.

Car sense

Remember to drive on the right, and be prudent at crossroads, roundabouts and when coming out of a petrol station. Speed limits are clearly marked on all roads in kilometres per hour. On most roads entering the Dordogne are large signs asking all visitors to keep the department *'propre'* (clean). Cars can be rented in Périgueux, Bergerac and Sarlat — for instance Budget Cars, 28 Rue Chanzy, Périgueux, tel. 53-09-88-48 or Citer, Route de Limoges, Trelissac, Tel. 53-03-97-50. Bicycles can be hired in the big towns and at the railway stations.

Widening your options

Although this book is primarily written for the independent traveller by car, or by car and caravan (see chapter on campsites), there are — fortunately — many alternatives. Many UK companies arrange conducted coach tours which provide an excellent introduction to the region. The only snag is the time spent getting to Dordogne and back. To give yourself a chance to discover the region you should allow at least 10 days in the Dordogne.

I have selected a wide range of alternatives, including 'thematic' holidays of interest to amateur and professional archaeologists, wine tasters, cooks, and rafting, canoe/kayak, painting, horseriding and language study holidays. There should be something here for everyone!

● **Car or fly/drive**

Cresta Holidays offer holidays in the Dordogne. 6 Acre House, Town Square, Sale M33 1SN, tel. 0345-056511. (11 nights from £405)

Inntravel offer motoring breaks to selected places in the Dordogne from £129. Hovingham, York Y06 4JZ, tel. 065-382741

Discover France, Badger Building, Oldmixon Cres., Weston-super-Mare, tel. 0934-620965

● Villas and country cottages

Allez France, Storrington RH20 4DZ, tel. 09066-5319

Sunvista Holidays, 5a George St. Warminster, Wiltshire BA12 8QA, tel. 0985-217444

Dominiques Villas, 2 Peterborough Mews, London SW6 3BL, tel. 01-736-1664

Just France. Prices are from £99 per house per week, exc. car ferry, or £143 inc. ferry

Eurovillas, 36 East St. Coggleshall, Colchester CO6 1SH, tel. 0376-61156

Sandpiper holidays, 34 Liverpool Rd, Liverpool L23 5UA, tel. 051-931-2826

● Hotel holidays

Slipaway Holidays, 90 Newland Rd. Worthing BN11 1LB, tel. 0903-821000. By car to Bergerac or Périgueux.

Just France, Eternit House, Felsham Rd, London SW15 1SF, tel. 01-788-3878. By air/car to Domme.

Sun-France, 3 Beaufort Gardens, London SW16 3BP, tel. 01-679-4562. By air/rail to Perigueux.

Cresta Holidays, 6 Acre House, Town Square, Sale M33 1SN, tel. 0345-056511. By air/car to St Cyprien.

VFB Holidays, 1 St Margaret Terrace, Cheltenham GL50 4DT, tel. 0242-526338. By air/car to Villefranche du Périgord.

France Voyages, 145 Oxford St. London W1R 1TB. To Beaulieu sur Dordogne or Bergerac. Tel. 01-494 3155

Example: Just France 7 nights half board cost £209, 15 days from £403 with holidays of the France Accueuil group.

● Coach tours

Epsom Coaches, Blenheim Rd, Epsom KT19 9AF, tel. 03727-27821.

HF Holidays offer Dordogne valley from £340. 142/4 Great North Way, London NW4 1EG, tel. 01-203-0433.

National Holidays, George House, George Street, Wakefield WF1 1LY, tel. 0924-383838.

● Château tours
Martin Sturge, Holiday in France, 3 Lower Camden Pl, Bath BA1 5JJ, tel. 0225-310623.
Page & May, 136-140 London Rd, Leicester LE2 1EN, tel. 0533-552521 offer tours of chateau country in the Dordogne (and the Loire).
Sandpiper Holidays, Sandpiper House, 34 Liverpool Rd, Liverpool L23 5UA, tel. 051-931-2826 offer château stays in the Dordogne.
Chapter Travel, 126 St Johns Wood High St, London NW8, tel. 01-586-9451.

● Café-Couette
Symot House, Henley on Thames, Oxon RG9 1XS, tel. 0491-578803 offer a national bed and breakfast service throughout France including the Dordogne.

● B & B Abroad
5 Worlds End Lane, Green Street Green, Orpington, Kent BR6 6AA. tel. 0689-55538.

● Farmhouses/villas
French Affair, 34 Lillie Rd. London SW6 1TH, tel. 01-381-8519.
Pleasurewood Holidays, Somerset House, Gordon Rd. Lowestoft NR22 1PZ, tel. 0502-517271 offer 7 night tours staying in up to 3 farms from £75.
Vacances en Campagne, Bignor, Pulborough, W. Sussex RH20 1QD, tel. 07987-292.
SBH France, Cavalier House, Tangmere, Chichester, W. Sussex, tel. 0243-773345.
Kingsland Holidays, 1 Pounds Park Rd, Plymouth PL2 4OP, tel. 0752-766822.

● Camping holiday
SVP France, 122 High St, Billingshurst, W. Sussex, RH14 8EP, tel. 040381-5165.

● Senior citizens

En Famille Agency (Overseas), The Old Stable, 60B Maltravers St, Arundel BN18 9BG, tel. 0903-883266. Home stays with a French family or houseparty centres in the Dordogne.

● Mobile homes

BCH Villafrance, tel. 0454-772410
SVP Holidays, see above.
Canvas Holidays, Bull Plain, Hertford SG14 1DY, tel. 0992-553535

● Rafting holidays

Pleasure Holidays, 11 Woodlands Rd. Northfield, Birmingham B31 2HU, tel. 021-475-2560 offer 2 weeks rafting along the Dordogne river from £136.
River Running Holidays, Wee Knochina'am, Portpatrick, Stranraer D69 9AD, Scotland, tel. 0776-81473 offer 100 miles of downstream rafting along the river Dordogne camping along the way, 2 weeks from £120.

● Painting holidays

British Airways Holidays, PO Box 100, Hodford House, 17-27 High St, Hounslow TW3 1TB, tel. 01-748-7559 offer 7 night holidays in the Dordogne from £467.
Susan & Guy Nicholls Painting Holidays, Belfrey House, Pain Hills, Cobham, Surrey offer painting in the Dordogne.

● Canoeing and sailing (also walks)

Country Special Holidays, 153b Kidderminster Rd, Bewdley DY12 1JE. tel. 0299-403528.
River Running Holidays, Wee Knochin'am, Portpatrick, Stranraer D69 9AD, tel. 0778-81473 offer luxury walking tours in the Dordogne. Two weeks from under £300.
Sunsites, Sunsite House, Station Rd, Dorking, Surrey RM4 1YZ, tel. 0306-887733 offer rambling holidays for campers in the Dordogne (and Loire) valley.
SVP Holidays see above.
Explore Worldwide, 7 High St, Aldershot GU11 1BH, tel. 0252-319448.

● Activity holidays

La France des Villages, Model Farm, Rattlesden, Bury St Edmunds IP30 0SY, tel. 0898-900900

● Horse riding and horsedrawn caravans

SVP Holidays, see above

Slipaway Holidays, 90 Newland Rd. Worthing BN11 1LB, tel. 0903-821000 offer 3-14 days holiday in horsedrawn caravans from £135.

● Cave paintings, archaeology

Callers Pegasus Travel, 3 Osborne Terrace, Newcastle upon Tyne NE2 1QD, tel. 091-281-4831 offer coach or air tours to the Dordogne.

Canvas Holidays, 9/13 Bull Plain, Hertford SG14 1DY, tel. 0992-553535 offer prehistory talks and trips to the Dordogne.

Country Special Holidays, 153b Kidderminster Rd, Bewdley DY12 1JE, tel. 0299-403528 offer 15 day prehistory tours to the Dordogne.

Francophiles – Discover France, 66 Great Brockeridge, Bristol BS9 3UA, tel. 0272-621975 offer 14 day coach tours with a cultural theme to the Dordogne from £550.

The Plantagenet Tours, 85 The Grove, Moordown, Bournemouth BH9 2TY, tel. 0202-521895 offer holidays to medieval France to visit Plantagenet country.

● Cookery courses and gastronomy

Country Special Tours see above, run gourmet cookery courses in Périgord and Quercy (Lot).

Francophiles – Discover France, see above, each year offer cookery courses and gastronomy in the Dordogne (and Brittany).

● Wine holidays

Eurocamp, Edmondson House, Tatton St Knutsford, Cheshire WA16 6BG, tel. 0565-3844 offer self drive camping and caravan holidays in the Bordeaux wine area.

Wessex Continental Travel, 124 North Road East, Plymouth PL4 6AH, tel. 0752-228333 offer wine holidays to the Dordogne (and Brittany) by coach.

● French language courses

Bonnes Vacances, Croes-y-Forwyn Uchaf, Eclwyswrw, Crymych, Dyfed SA4 3PR, tel. 023979-665 offer French language courses in a domestic setting in the Dordogne from £150 per week.

En Famille Agency, The Old Stable, 60b Maltravers St, Arundel BN18 9BG, tel. 0903-883266 have language courses in the Dordogne.

AAL, 9 Haywra St, Harrogate, York HG1 5BJ, tel. 0423-505313.

Ciel in France (J.L.Lefevre), Chateau de la Valouze, 24490 La Roche Chalais, Dordogne, tel. 010-33-53-91-44-28.

Euroacademy, 77A George St. Croydon CR0 1CD, tel. 01-682-6000.

● Cycling

Susi Madrone 'Cycling for Softies'.

Lloyds House, 22 Lloyds St, Manchester M2 5WA, tel. 061-834 6800

SVP France, 122 High St. Billingshurst, W. Sussex, tel. 040381-5165

Headwater, Northwich, Cheshire CW8 3BR, tel. 0606-782011.

France Individuelle, 122 High St. Billingshurst, W. Sussex RH14 8EP, tel. 040-381-5166

● Walking holidays

River Running Holidays, see above

SVP France as above

Waymark Holidays, 295 Lillie Rd, London SW6 7LL, tel. 01-385-5015

Ron and Jenny Farmer who run Francophiles, offer two special tours to the Dordogne each year; 'Spring in the Dordogne', and in the autumn 'Landscapes of the Dordogne' with prices of £450-£600. The latter's itinerary left on a Sunday from Bristol and thence by bus to Roye, Versailles, Chartres to Loches. In the Dordogne area there were visits to Martel, Saint Cére (Hotel du Coq Arlequin). Also visits to Beynac castle, La Roque-Gageac and Domme bastide. Then

Carennac, Beaulieu-sur-Dordogne, Collonges-la-Rouge, Autoire and Rocamadour (outside the Dordogne dept), Cahors (in the Lot), Sarlat, Souillac, Padirac, Bellac, St Savin, and home via Loches, Chenonceaux, Orleans and Vimy.

Falcon Holidays, 33 Notting Hill Gate, London W11 3JQ, tel. 01-221-8454 offer a week's rental of a Dordogne gite for £66, alternatively rent the thirteenth century mill with drawbridge in Lustrac.

Eurovillas offer old houses or villas in St Germain-des-Belvès south west of Sarlat near Les Eyzies, large enough for seven people, at £415 per week in low season, £500 in mid-season and £610 in high season. (Ref. FR8/10/1).'

Methods of travel

● Air
From Paris there are flights to Périgueux and Bergerac. Two flights per day taking one and a half hours.

● Train
Frequent trains from Paris to Périgueux take four hours, from Toulouse three hours, from Bordeaux one and a quarter hours and from Lyon five hours.

● Car
Paris is 500 km from Périgueux — the quickest route is the *autoroute* Paris-Orleans, then the N20 Orleans — Limoges and N21 Limoges — Périgueux. The alternative route is the autoroute Paris — Poitiers, then N10 — Angoulême and D939 Angouleme to Périgueux.

Top twenty places in the Dordogne

The most beautiful town	Sarlat 'vieux ville'
The most beautiful villages	(1) St Jean de Cole (2) St Leon sur Vézère (3) Carennac (Lot)

The most outstanding natural wonder	Padirac underground chasm and caverns
The most elegant small town	Brantôme with its rivers and abbey
The most elegant castle	Jumilhac-le-Grand
The best aggressive military fortresses	(1) Beynac (2) Castelnau-Bretenoux (Lot)
The most interesting castle, architecturally	Biron with five different styles
The grandest château	Hautefort (now fully repaired)
The best wine tasting château/museum	Monbazillac
The best kept bastide town	Monpazier in the valley
The most beautiful bastide town	Domme on a craggy hill
The most dramatic religious site	Rocamadour hanging on the cliffside
My favourite abbey	Cadouin and its cloisters
The classic fortified abbey-church	Saint-Amand-de-Coly
The best 'jardin publique'	Sarlat
The prehistoric sites	A dozen around les Eyzies-de-Tayac
The best troglodyte village	La Madeleine (Tursac)
The best selection of Roman remains	Périgueux

The best selection of wines	Bergerac wine co-op near the station
The most interesting museum	Musée du Périgord, Périgueux (closed Tuesday)
The best musical festival	St Léon de Vézère, a whole week in early August

CHAPTER THREE:
GREEN DORDOGNE

The Dordogne offers more than most other French regions to the 'green' visitors. This chapter is for the adventurers, the romantics and the water lovers. For the active there are cycling holidays, walking on the Grandes Randonnées, riding holidays and potholing. For the romantic there are 'roulotte à cheval' holidays where you can hire a four-wheeled horse driven caravan to clop-clop along the minor roads exploring the countryside. For water buffs there are details of canoeing/kayak holidays on the great, majestic, smooth-flowing rivers.

Walking holidays *(Randonnées pedestres)*

The Dordogne is excellent walking country. The French take their long distance walking very seriously. Their *'Grandes Randonnées* are well-marked tracks crossing France in all directions. The G.R. No. 6 starts in the west and comes through St Foy-la-Grande, Monbazillac, Tremolat, Limeuil, Le Bugue, Les Eyzies-de-Tayac, Sarlat, towards Souillac and Rocamadour. The G.R.64 goes from Les Eyzies-de-Tayac, St Cyprien, Allas, to Domme, Grojelac and Vitrac, east towards Payrac and Rocamadour.

    The G.R.36 comes into the Dordogne in the north west at La Rochebeaucourt, Mareuil, Bourdeilles, Chancelade, north of Périgueux, towards Montignac, Thonac, and St Léon de Vézère. The G.R.4 crosses the north of the department at Busserolles, to Bussière Badil, Piégut-Pluviers and Abjat sur Bandiat. You can just follow the routes on the Michelin map No. 75, but keen walkers can buy detailed local Topoguides in French (some in English from McCarta Ltd. 122 Kings Cross Road, London WC1X 9DS, tel. 01-278-8276). Ramblers Holidays, Box 43, Welwyn Garden City, Herts AL8 6PQ, tel. 0707-331133 offer walking parties in the Dordogne.

If you don't want to backpack you could rent an ass provided you are prepared to sweet-talk, feed and water it. An ass can cover 10-20 km at 3-4 km/hour (heavily laden) each day. There are various 'Ass Circuits' around Les Eyzies – Le Bugue. A week's rental costs 850 francs and each animal can carry equipment for three or four people. Details from the Périgueux tourist office or S.I. at Le Bugue, tel. 53-06-20-48.

Cycling holidays

Three UK companies organise cycle-touring holidays in France:-

- Bike Tours, P.O. Box 75, Bath B1A 1BX, tel. 0225-65786
- Pedals Adventure Cycle Expeditions, 101 Eland Rd, London SW11, tel. 01-223-7922
- Susi Madrons Cycling Holidays, Lloyds House, 22 Lloyds St, Manchester M2 5WA, tel. 061-834 6800

Rob Hunter, in his book 'Cycle Touring in France' recommends a two week cycle tour of the Dordogne averaging 80 km per day, which starts at Périgueux. First stop due north Chancelade (abbey), Brantôme (abbey, truffles and rivers), west to Bourdeilles castle, Riberac (romanesque churches, foie gras and summer concerts), Saint Aulaye (splendid fairs on April 30th and May 1st), La Roche Chalais (lakes and wild boars), west and a sneaky look at Capet and St Emilion (superb wines) just in the Charente Maritime department. Castillon-la-Bataille (where the 100 Years War ended in humiliating defeat for the English army), past Montaigne's château (his library is one of the literary 'views' of France), east to Bergerac (wines and tobacco museums), south to Monbazillac (château and white wine) into bastide country. Eymet, Issigeac, Villeréal, a little dogleg to see mighty Biron's castle and to the best bastide of Monpazier. North east to Cadouin (abbey), Lalinde on the river Dordogne (an English bastide town and Bergerac wine production), along the river Vézère valley, Cingle de Tremolat, Pont Coude to Les Eyzies (grottos and prehistory museum) and to Montignac (Lascaux II and prehistory museum). South along the D704 to Sarlat. Next follows a spell through enchanted castle territory, Beynac, Castelnaud, Domme and Montfort. Finally Rob

Hunter entices the cyco-tourist out of the Dordogne via Souillac to Rocamadour, Martel and Brive-la-Gaillarde.

On arrival at Périgueux bicycles can be hired at Cumenal-Huot, 41 bis Cours St Georges, tel. 53-53-31-56. There are cycling clubs in many parts of the Dordogne including Mussidan, Sarlat, Lalinde, Monpazier, Montpon-Ménéstrol. The French take their *'vélo'* riding very seriously. Loisirs Acceuil, c/o the tourist office in Périgueux, 16 Rue Wilson, tel. 53-53-44-35, have arranged three tours called *'Le Périgord à vélo'* for groups of up to 10 riders (over 12 years old). The package includes cycle rental, topo-guide, demi-pension, separate transport for luggage and a tent. One week's tour, Marquay − Sarlat, averages 30 km per day and costs about 1200 francs. Another three day guided tour of the prehistory area costs about 700 francs per person. The whole tour is theoretically 620 km, but there are temptations to make excursions so a realistic total is about 700 km altogether.

French Rail (SNCF) operate a national rent-a-bicycle service known as *'Train et vélo'* which operates from 250 stations in France including Sarlat, Bergerac, Les Eyzies, Belvès and Lalinde.

Cycles can also be rented from:

Location	Name	Tel.
Monpazier	M. Mouret	53-22-63-46
Bergerac	M. Mazeau, 11 Pl. Gambetta	53-57-07-19
	M. Seurin, 114 Bd. de l'Entrepot	53-57-71-99
Les Eyzies	Syndicat d'Initiative	53-06-97-05
Montignac	Cycles Ricros, 27 Rue IV Septembre	53-51-87-02
Périgueux	Cycles Germagnan,	
	96 Av. Maréchal Juin	53-53-41-91
	M. Cumenal, 41 bis Cours St Georges	53-53-31-56
Riberac	M. Lissandreau, 85 Rue 26 Mars 1944	53-90-16-30
Sarlat	Au Vélo Dingo, Pl. André Malraux	53-31-00-93
	Garage Matigot, 52 Av. Gambetta	53-59-03-60
	Périgord Moto, Rte. de Souillac	53-59-42-95
Montpon	M. Merilhou, 25 Rue Wilson	53-80-37-34
Thiviers	M. Bruyère, 31 bis Rue Lamy	53-55-05-69

Local cycle tours

L'Aventure à Vélo, La Garrigue, St André-d'Allas, just west of Sarlat on the D25, 24200 Sarlat, tel. 53-31-24-18, offer several inclusive *vélo* tours. One is a week with half board in the Vézère valley biking your way to all the grottos and castles. Including transport of luggage (and a tent if you choose to stay on a campsite) plus local topoguide it costs 1214 francs on campsite, 1738 francs if in a two star hotel. Available between 15th April and 15th September. Another alternative is on a high performance 18 speed mountain bike which costs 2174 francs for full board for a week. Have a go! Cyclo-Cross children's bikes are available too. A standard bike costs 55 francs per day.

True green

The Herbarium or garden of medicinal plants in Les Eyzies, tel. 53-06-97-24, has over 200 trees, shrubs and plants with medical properties.

Horses

Besides hiring a Périgourdin nag *'roulotte à cheval'* with caravan there are a score of official *'centres equestres'* i.e. recognised riding stables catering for the tourist. They all offer a range of services and programmes, including lessons if required. *'Haras'* is French for horse breeding stables. I have grouped them roughly north to south with the name of the stable manager to whom you should write for a brochure.

● Northern region

Sarrazac, 24800 Thiviers, Club Hippique de Château, tel. 53-55-06-32 (G. Boyer)

Puyrenier, 24340 Mareuil-Belle, Relais Equestre Domaine de Bellevue (Bouskela)

Festalemps 24410, 10 km west of Riberac, La Double au Rythme du Cheval, Moulin de la Gacherie, tel. 53-90-09-42 (Faivre). A two day weekend costs 750 francs, a week in high season 2700 francs. You get a well-trained horse, two large saddlebags, insurance, horse fodder, bed & breakfast and supper for 6 nights.

● Central region

Périgueux, 24430 Coursac, Rando-Cheval-Plus, Ferme du Petit Cerf, tel. 53-08-78-29 (Michel)

Périgueux, 24000, Etrier Périgordin, Domaine de Borie-Petit (Laurençon), tel. 53-53-61-48

Atur, Route de Pommier, Haras de Bagnac, tel. 53-53-28-73

Trelissac, Cravache de Trellissac, Poney-Club, tel. 53-08-14-58

St Laurent-des-Hommes, Cheval nature, Beauperier, 24400 Mussidan, tel. 53-81-75-00 (Bessou)

Vergt 24380, Ferme Equestre de Boutazac, Rte de Bergerac (22 km S of Périgueux) tel. 53-54-97-00 (Bourland)

● South west region

St Sauveur, 24520 Mouleydier, Poney club Hippique, tel. 53-27-20-56 (Hergat) (east of Bergerac on river)

Boisse, 24560 Issigeac, Ranch El Corral, tel. 53-58-75-36 (Jubertie)

Faux, 24560 Issigeac, Babette et Philippe, Metairie du Roc, tel. 53-24-32-57 (Aguesse)

Mazeyrolles, 24550 (east of Monpazier) Ranch de Mazeyrolles, tel. 53-29-93-38 (Marescassier)

Monpazier 24540, Centre Equestre de Marsalès, tel. 53-22-63-14 (Cassang). Hire and upmarket holiday for a week staying and eating in a two star hotel costs 3950 francs.

● South centre

Alles sur Dordogne 24480, Ranch de la Vallée, tel. 53-22-08-56 (Fournier). A week costs 1400 francs excluding food and lodging.

Urval, 24480 Le Buisson, Ferme de Pessel, tel. 53-22-09-46 (Verspieren)

Tursac, 24620 Les Eyzies, Centre Equestre de la Baronie, tel. 53-06-93-83 (Viseur)

● South east region

Castelnaud-les-Milandes 24250, Club Hippique, La Vallée des Châteax − La Treille, tel. 53-29-51-86 (Rouzier)

St Antoine-deBreuilh 24230, Eperon Laurentais, Les Laurents, tel. 53-24-80-36 (Prunis)

Sarlat 24200, Club Hippique Fournier-Sarlovèze, Bonnefond, Rte, de Vezac, tel. 53-59-15-83 (Orvain)

A number of villages have riding events and competitions:

● St Jean-de-Côle, south east of Nontron, seasonal horse races.

● St Pierre de Chignac south east of Périgueux has a notable breeding 'haras' stables.

● St Pardou-de-Dronne, east of Riberac has good horse trails.

● St Antoine-Cumond near Riberac has summer competitions, 'concours hippique'.

● Prats du Périgord, south of Belvès, has summer equestrian rallies.

● Paunat, north of Tremolat, has organised horse 'promenades'.

● Brantôme has summer horse riding compeititions.

● Marsales near Monpazier has a 'hippodrome', equitation arena for competitions.

● Mensignac, west of Périgueux has special riding paths and tracks.

Pot-holing or spéléologie

The Dordogne has a wealth of deep caves and rock shafts variously known as Gouffres, Igues, Aven, Cloup or Sotch in the old vernacular. There are a number of interesting sites for the intrepid to tackle. At Les Eyzies there is the Musée de la Spéléologie, open 1st July to 31st August except Saturdays, tel. 53-29-68-42. The museum is actually in the rock fortress of Tayac, with four large display chambers. This is a sensible place to start since they have plans and maps of the main pot-holing sites in the Dordogne — and here are some of them.

Bayac (pop. 300) is a small village on the D660 4 km south of Lalinde with pot-holes in the valley of the river Couze.

Beaumont (pop. 1300) is a large village 6 km south of Bayac also on the river Couze. It is a bastide on a hill with a fortified romanesque church, lots of Bergerac wine and the super castle of Bannes just north on the D660.

Couze et Saint Front (pop. 1000) is in the valley where the river Couze meets the river Dordogne just opposite Lalinde. This is troglodyte country with many *'cluzeaux'*, grottos and the prehistoric Trou (hole) du Peyrol.

Saint Astier (pop. 4100) is a town on the N89 20 km south west from Périgueux in the valley of the river Isle, with several pot-hole sites.

Bourdeilles (pop. 650) is a prehistoric village north west of Périgueux with a famous chateau and superb views over the river Dronne. In the rock faces on the way to Brantôme is La Forge du Diable, and, where the Dronne meets the river Boulou, the *'gouffre'* called *'Puits de Fontas'*. Ask at the *Syndicat d'Initiative* for local pot-hole sites.

Cubjac (pop. 600) is a village on the river Auvézère east of Périgueux with neolithic *'gisements'* and the Gouffre du Moulin des Soucis where the Auvézère river flows underground to rejoin the river l'Isle.

Saint Martin des Combes (pop. 150) is a hamlet north east of Bergerac and east of the N21, on the river Caudau. Local *'cluzeaux'* are called Grange-Neuve, Farinéras, la Bessède and des Cluzettes.

Saint Perdoux (pop. 150) is a hamlet on the N21, south of Bergerac, and the pot-hole is called *'cluzeau aux Crambes'*.

Tremolat (pop. 500) is a village with superb views of the Dordogne valley, east of Lalinde. Prehistoric sites include Roquebégude, Lestruque and Soulalève. Ask for details at the *Syndicat de'Initiative*.

Sainte-Mondane (pop. 250) is in the valley of the Dordogne near the château of Fénelon, 25 km south east of Sarlat. Lovely panoramas.

Terrasson-la-Villedieu (pop. 6250) is a town 60 km due east of Périgueux, on the N89 in the valley of the river Vézère.

The 'gouffre des Soudes', the rocks and grotto of St Sour, and the prehistoric site of Genoliac produce several pot-holing possibilities. The syndicat d'initiative will advise you.

Cunèges (pop. 200) is a hamlet south east of Bergerac where the rivers Gardonnette and Bessage join. Prehistoric *cluzeaux* and underground caves produce local pot-holing 'caves'.

Montignac (pop. 3100) is one of the centres of prehistory. Lascaux is only 3 km away, as in Regourdin and Gaulejac. Ask at the town hall for advice on several sites in the Vézère valley.

Campagne (pop. 220) is in the valley of the Vézère halfway between Le Bugue and Les Eyzies. Prehistoric 'gisements' abound called 'Roc-de-Marsal' and 'La Vergnole', and the grotto 'Trou-du-Chien'.

Audrix (pop. 120) is a hamlet south of Le Bugue. Just to the north is the famous Gouffre de Proumeyssac by the valley rocks of the Vézère, one of the most popular rock 'holes' in the Dordogne.

Le Fleix (pop. 1250) is a small town in the valley of the river Dordogne 6 km north east of Sainte Foy-la-Grande on the D20. Wine from the co-op will warm you up after a pot-holing stint.

Bouzic (pop. 150) is a hamlet in the valley of the river Céou, 12 km south fo Domme, with gorttos, subterranean lakes and rivers and the 'Trou du Vent'.

Deglan (pop. 630) is a village also in the Céou valley 3 km north west of Bouzic. There are waterfalls and grottos.

One of the main pot-holing clubs in the Dordogne is in Périgueux at 38 Rue du 26 Regiment d'Infanterie (a suitable martial address!) tel. 53-53-46-50. They can advise you where to find the local clubs in the various regions. It is essential to get advice, help and assistance on the spot before tackling the unknown holes and to make sure you leave a message with someone giving them details of your plans just in case something goes wrong.

Horse-drawn caravans

A few of the French rural departments including Gascony and the Dordogne cultivate the gentle, peaceful holiday pastime of horse-drawn caravanning. A one day tour 10.30 a.m.-6 p.m. costs 495 francs per family. For one, two or three weeks a family of two adults, or two adults plus one or two children can rent a horse-drawn four-wheeled caravan from one of three bases within a 50 km radius of Périgueux. The season is April to October and 2, 3, 4 or 5 day weekend rentals are possible. The high season is from 1st July to the end of August and the weekly rental is 3700 francs; in low season (25th March to 30th June, and 26th August to 16th October) rental is 2300 francs for the first week and 1800 francs for additional weeks. Two day weekends start at 1000 francs. The main booking office is Service de Reservation Loisirs Accueil, 16 Rue Wilson, 24009 Périgueux, tel. 53-53-44-35. In the UK Slipaway Holidays can book you a *roulotte* holiday, tel. 0903-821000.

There are two circuits:
- The bastide route south east of Bergerac covering Monpazier — St Avit Rivière — St Avit-Sénieur — Beaumont — Naussanes — Issigeac — Boisse — Ste-Sabine — Rampieux and back to Monpazier. The route is a figure of eight covering about 100 km.
- The northern route covers Brantôme — St Pierre de Côle — St Jean de Côle — Villars — Quinsac — St Pardoux-la-Rivière — east of Nontron — Champs Romain — Abjat-sur-Bandiat Piégut — west to Javerlhac and back on a different route to Brantôme. About 150 km with plenty of châteaux and abbeys to see. Beauvinière in Quinsac is a booking centre.

The horse is well trained, knows the route, travels at 6 km per hour, and becomes your friend (and responsibility). A five page horse 'maintenance' manual is provided, plus three pages of advice to you the driver. The caravan sleeps four and is fully equipped with cooking facilities. A bicycle is recommended for off-road tours. One month before your booking commences you will be sent a full brief, itineraries, practical guide, list of places to stay etc. Incidentally the horse is **NOT** to be ridden, he is just a friendly plodder.

Calèches

For the less adventurous why not try a horse-drawn open
carriage. You can rent one of these for the day. It takes 4-5
people for 496 francs, from 10.30 a.m. to 6 p.m. Attelages
du Périgord, Mazeyrolles, 24550 Villefranche du Périgord, tel.
53-29-98-99.

Helicopter tours

The Sarlat-Domme aerodrome, tel. 53-28-24-36, offers a
variety of helicopter tours based on four passengers. A half
hour's close inspection either of a 32 châteaux circuit, or to
Rocamadour plus 17 châteaux, will set you back 540 francs
per person. A shorter flight around Domme looking at the
valley of the river Dordogne and three châteaux costs 150
francs per person. They also have a pilot-training school.
Local flights can be made from Périgueux-Bassillac airport, tel.
53-54-41-19 and from Bergerac-Roumanières, tel.
53-57-31-36.

Hot air ballooning (south east of Sarlat)

Called Montgolfier after the original intrepid inventor of this
curious sport, one can have a weekend in July-August for
2400 francs at the château of Veyrignac in its 20 hectare park.
During the ritzy weekend you get a 1½ hour 'vol' in the
balloon (which holds eight people), a candlelit dinner in the
old room at the château, and you sleep in a 'lit à baldaquin'.
Information from tourist offices, Périgueux or Sarlat.

Parachuting holiday

The parachuting club is based at the Bergerac aerodrome. A
week's holiday between February and October costs 3150
francs for a beginner (plus 1600 francs for the instructor who
jumps with you). For that you get half board and lodging,
parachute rental and five jumps. Alternatively you can pay
4100 francs and get the same week's half board, lodging,
training and 10 jumps. You can enjoy a marvellous aerial view
of the vineyards but you need to have a medical checkup by
the local doctor before being allowed to join the club. There
are also aeroclubs at Sarlat-Domme, Belvès, Riberac, St

Pardoux-Vielvic, Port Sainte-Foy, La Rochebeau, Bergerac and Périgueux.

Golfing holiday

Special golfing groups (8–40) can have a week's play at the nine hole course of Lolivarie, staying at the Auberge de la Petite Reine. The rates vary considerably, and it is much cheaper out of season. Beginners can have 20 hours of tuition and *pension complet* for 3900 francs per week in high season. Another nine hole course is in the grounds of the Chateau de Sadillac, 12 km south of Bergerac, tel. 53-58-46-09. Yet another course outside Périgueux is at Saltgourde.

Water, water everywhere

The several large rivers which cross the Dordogne make it an ideal holiday for parents with children. Besides the long, wide, gently flowing rivers such as the Dordogne, Vézère, Isle, Vergt, Dronne and Auvézère, there are a score of *'plans d'eau'* or man-made lakes. These are usually sited just outside a village and provide excellent bathing facilities for all ages, including toddlers. There will probably be 'en tout cas' tennis courts, beaches for alfresco picnics, as well as trees for shade from the hot mid-summer sun. There are also large natural lakes, for instance Saint-Estèphe, near Augignac north of Nontron. Most of the lakes have nearby camping facilities.

I include in the following table facilities for canoeing or kayak in the region. There are over 200 km of rivers without dams or *'barrages'* and several firms offer two to seven day canoe holidays with tent and mattress, life-belts, insurance, canoe rental and return by bus to the original starting point. Tarifs are about 170 francs per person per day, but a week's rental is much less − 475 francs or 66 francs per day (excluding meals).

1) Canoe-Raid, Siorac-en-Périgord, 24170 Belvès, tel. 53-31-64-11
2) Roquegeoffre location canoe, St Vincent de Losse, 24220 St Cyprien, tel. 53-29-54-20

3) Canoe à Cenac, 'Randonnée Dordogne', 24250 Domme, tel. 53-28-22-01
4) Le Sioux, Pont de Cenac, tel. 53-28-30-81
5) Canoes Loisirs, 24200 Vitrac, tel. 53-28-23-43

Also from Montignac you can book canoes for the descent of the river Vézère and from St Mesmin (north of Hautefort) a descent of the river Auvézère south west towards Périgueux.

A Scots firm offer excellent rafting holidays on the Dordogne, starting at Argentat on the river Dordogne 30 km north of St Céré. The two man rubber boats (larger ones for groups) drift or are paddled, often over rapids, westwards via Beaulieu, Carennac, Florac and Castlenaud. Tents are provided for overnight stays along the riverside. Information from River Runners, Wee Knochin'am, Portpatrick, Wigtownshire DG9 9AD, tel. 0776-81473.

Boating tours start from either Beynac or La Roque-Gageac in traditional fishing boats called *'gabarres'*. The trips over 7½ km, last one hour and cost 30 francs (children half price). Information from P.H. Keller, St Martial de Nabirat, 24250 Domme, tel. 53-28-51-15, or Les Norbert, La Roque-Gageac, tel. 53-59-47-48. English commentaries, and binoculars are provided to study the several castles you will see from the river trip. There are other boating tours from the so-called *'port'* at Bergerac to see the dam down river. Duration 1-2 hours, tel 53-57-02-31. Also from the *centre-nautique* at Tremolat at 5 p.m. in mid-summer for one and a half hours to see the *'Cingle de Tremolat'*, the river loop with notable castles. Tarif 40 francs per person.

If you are a keen fisherman every local information office or town hall will tell you how to join the fishing club (you need a permit to catch fresh water fish — trout, roach, perch, bream, pike, tench and carp). Some of the best fishing lakes are around Nontron (Étang de Saint-Estéphe) and in the Double and Landais.

Many villages have near Olympic standard swimming pools, usually with separate children's pools. On the river there are bathing 'beaches' or *'baignades'*, often near the local camping site.

Facilities

Environs of Périgueux	Bathing	Sailing	Canoe/ Kayak
Antonne-et-Trigonant (NE)	x	x	
Bassilac (E)		x	x
Bourdeilles (NW)			x
Brantôme	Pool		x
Cherveix-Cubas (NE)	x		Base
Coulares (NE)	x	x	
La Douze (SE)	x	x	
Grignols (SE)	x		
Hautefort (NE)	Artificial lake		
Lisle	x		x
Marsac-sur-L'Isle (W)			x
Mayac (NE)	x		x
Montpon-Ménéstrol (SW)	Pool	x	x
Montrem (SW)			x
Mussidan (SW)	Pool	x	x
Nailhac (E)		x	x
Neuvic (SW)	Artificial lake		x
Périgueux	Pool		x
Razac-sur-L'Isle (W)	x	x	x
Saint-Astier (SW)	Artificial lake	x	x
Saint-Aquiln (W)	Artificial lake		x
St Léon-sur-L'Isle (SW)	x		x
St Vincent-sur-L'Isle (NE)	x	x	
Sarliac-sur-L'Isle (NE)	x		x
Tocane-Saint-André (NW)	x		
Trelissac (N)			x
Near Dordogne river west-east			
Saint-Seurin-de-Prats	x	x	
Saint-Antoine-de-Breuilh			x
Porte-Sainte-Foy	x	x	x
Le Fleix	x		
Lamonzie-St-Martin	x		x

	Bathing	Sailing	Canoe/ Kayak
Bergerac	Pool	Club	
Mouleydier			x
Lalinde	Pool		x
Badefols-sur-Dordogne	x	x	x
Mauzac-et-Grand Castaing	x	x	
Allès-sur-Dordogne	x		
Tremolat	Artificial lake	x	
Berbiguières			x
Coux-et-Bigaroque			x
Siorac-en-Périgord	x	x	
Le Buisson-de-Cadouin	x		
Saint Cyprien	x		
Bezenac			x
Beynac-et-Cazenac	x	x	x
La Roque-Gageac	x		x
Vitrac	x	x	
Cenac-et-St Julien	x	x	x
Domme	Pool		
Calviac-en-Périgord	x		
Carlux	x		
Cazoulès	x		
Peyrillac et Millas	x		x
Environs of Sarlat			
Le Bugue (W)	Pool	x	
La Cassagne (NE)	Artificial lake		x
Daglan(S)	x	x	x
Limeuil (W)	x	x	
Montignac (N)			x
Saint-Cybranet (S)			x
Saint-Geniès (NE)	x		
Terrasson-la-Villedieu (NE)	Pool		
Villefranche du Périgord (S)	x		
Environs of Bergerac			
Sigoulès (SW)	Artificial lake		

	Bathing	Sailing	Canoe/ Kayak
Carsac-de-Gurson (W)	Artificial lake	x	
Faux (SE)		x	
Issigeac (SE)	Artificial lake		
Environs of Riberac			
Villetoureix (NE)			x
Saint-Aulaye (W)	Pool		
Riberac town	Pool	x	
Montagrier (E)	x		
La Jemaye (S)	x	x	
Echourgnac (SW)	x	x	
Comberanche et Epalache (W)		x	
Near Nontron			
Busserolles (N)	x		
Jumilhac-le-Grand (E)	x		x
Mialet (E on river Côle)	Artificial lake	x	
Champagnac-de-Belair (S)	Pool		x
Vieux Mareuil (SW)	Artificial lake	x	
Piegut-Pluviers (N)	x		
Saint-Estèphe (N)	Artificial lake	x	
St Pardoux-la-Rivière (E)	x	x	
St Saud-Lacoussière (?)	Artificial lake	x	
Thiviers (SE)	Pool		x
Savignac-Ledrier (S of Thiviers)	x		x
Salagnac (SE of Thiviers)	Artificial lake		
Angoisse (NE of Thiviers)	Artificial lake	x	
Payzac (E of Thiviers)			x

Note: x = Facilities available

CHAPTER FOUR:
ACCOMMODATION OFF THE BEATEN TRACK

If you and your family *must* visit the Dordogne in peak season (for school holidays or any other reason) then there is an alternative to the busy crowded five main towns and the campsites. Remember the French themselves are dedicated campers and the sites will be full unless you reserve a month or more before your visit.

Budget hotels

I would recommend that you choose the one or two star hotels with restaurants, in one, or more, of the score of little villages mentioned in this chapter. That way you will enjoy your holiday without the pressures of overcrowded campsites. You should write in French I'm afraid, but see draft letter and ask for demi-pension or, if you have a hungry tribe, full pension terms for a stay of three days or longer.

Draft Letter

Mardi, le 5 Mai 19——
[insert correct date]

Monsieur,

Ayant obtenu votre addresse par l'entremise du Guide pour la Dordogne, nous envisageons de séjourner dans votre établissement et serions heureux de connaître vos conditions pour demi pension/pension pour deux/trois/ quatre personnes [delete as appropriate] *au mois de* [insert date] *pour quelques jours dans une chambre simple avec W.C./sans W.C/avec douche/sans douche* [delete as appropriate].

Avec nos remerciements, nous vous prions d'agréer, Monsieur, l'expression de nos salutations distinguées

[Signature]

Most of the little villages and small towns which I list have
castles, rivers, *piscines,* *plans d'eaux* (man-made swim-
ming/boating centres in the countryside) and grottos within
easy reach. *Demi-pension* terms should cost in the region of
150 francs per person per day on the basis of two people per
room. Most will have their own 'parking', gardens, and menus
at about 50 francs. I have grouped them into seven areas.

● South east around Sarlat

Tel.

24170	Belvès (south west) Hôtel de France, 1 Av. Paul-Crampel	53-29-11-80
24170	Siorac (south west) Hôtel le Trefle à Quatre Feuilles	53-31-60-26
24250	Grolejac (nr Domme) Hôtel du Pont	53-28-15-94
24620	Les Eyzies (west) Hôtel Le Périgord	53-06-97-26
24480	Le Buisson de Cadouin (south west) HR des Voyageurs	53-22-90-64
24250	Bouzic (nr Domme) Hôtel Sylvestre	53-28-41-01
24260	St Alvère (west) Hôtel La Boule d'Or, 29 Rue République	53-22-70-26
24250	St Cybranet (South nr Domme) Hôtel Beau Rivage	53-28-32-13
24120	Terrasson-La-Villedieu (north) Hôtel Willer	53-50-06-93

● West around Riberac-Mussidan

24410	St Aulaye Hôtel du Champ de Foire	53-90-82-29
24600	Riberac Hôtel de la Gare (no rest.)	53-90-01-00
24400	Mussidan Hôtel Grand Café, 1 Av. Gambetta	53-81-00-07
24400	Mussidan Hôtel des Voyagers, 40 Rue Libération	53-81-00-12
24700	Montpon-Ménéstrol Hôtel Saint-Eloi	53-82-23-93
24700	Montpon-Ménéstrol Le Port Vieux	53-80-32-18
24440	Montferrand HR Lou Peyrol	53-22-33-63
24400	Beauronne Hôtel Le Combiaou	53-80-00-72
24400	Sourzac Hôtel Le Croquant (La Gravete N 89)	53-81-11-74

		Tel.
24210	Thenon Hôtel Chez Serge	53-15-20-31
24140	Douville (East of Mussidan) Hôtel du Midi	53-82-98-04

● The South West not too far from Bergerac

24220	St Cyprien (east) Le Petit Chaperon Rouge, Coux et Bigaroque	53-31-60-48
24680	Gardonne (west) Le St. Michel, Av. du Périgord	53-27-89-22
24130	La Force (west) Hostellerie des Ducs	53-58-95-63
24520	Mouleydier (east) Auberge Beau Rivage, Rte de Sarlat	53-23-20-21
24560	Bouniagues (south east) Hôtel des Voyageurs	53-58-32-26
24510	Limeuil Haut (east) Au Bon Acceuil	53-22-03-19
24100	Lembras (north east) Relais de la Ribeyrie, N 21	53-27-02-92
24440	Beaumont (east south east) Les Arcades (inexpensive)	53-22-30-31
24440	Beaumont (east south east) Chez Popaul	53-22-30-11
24140	St Georges de Monclard (north east) Le Bon Coin	53-82-98-47
24140	St Georges de Monclard (north east) Hôtel Lambert	53-82-98-56
24260	Audrix (nr Le Bugue) Auberge Medievale	53-07-24-02
24510	Mauzac et Grand Castang (nr Lalinde) HR du Barrage	53-22-50-56
24500	Eymet (south) Hôtel Beauséjour, Bd. National	53-23-81-25
24500	Eymet (south) Hôtel du Château, 9 Rue du Couvent	53-23-81-35
24220	Coux et Bigaroque (nr St Cyprien) HR La Cotte de Mailles	53-31-61-04

● Centre around Montignac

24290	Aubas (north east) Hôtel L'Arzeme	53-51-81-20
24210	Auriac (north west) Hôtel Sarlat (D67)	53-51-86-29
24210	Auriac (north west) Hôtel Le Laurence (D67)	53-51-84-81

Tel.

24290	Montignac Le Perigord	53-51-80-38
24290	Montignac La Grotte	53-51-80-48
24290	Montignac Le Bon Acceuil	53-51-82-95
24590	Saint-Genies (south east) Relais des Tourists, Croix de la Borie	53-28-97-60
24290	St Léon sur Vézère (south) Auberge du Pont (pretty village)	53-50-73-07
24290	Le Moustier (south) Hôtel Les Vignes	53-50-72-51
24290	La Chapelle-Aubareil, Hôtel du Jardin	53-50-79-99

● Centre around Périgueux

24750	Champcevinal (north) Hôtel La Forge	53-04-61-65
24000	Nôtre Dame de Sanilhac, Auberge Notre Dame	53-07-60-69
24420	Sarliac/L'Isle (north east) Hôtel Le Nordoc	53-07-83-61
24420	Sarliac/L'Isle (north east) Hôtel Chabrol	53-06-01-35
24750	Lesparparat-Boulazac (south east) Hôtel Formule 1	53-08-62-00
24110	Saint-Astier (south west) Hôtel de Paris	53-54-10-20
24110	Saint Astier (south west) La Terrasse de Chassaing	53-54-12-00
24110	St Léon-sur-L'Isle (south west) La Ferme des Iles	53-80-64-90
24100	Bassillac (east) Hôtel L'Escale	53-54-42-95
24100	Boulazac (south east) Hôtel Le Relax	53-09-31-28
24380	Vergt (south) Hôtel du Parc, Pl. Marty	53-54-90-50

● The North around Nontron

24390	Badefols-d'Ans (nr Hautefort) HR les Tilleuls	53-51-52-97
24530	Champagnac du Bel Air (south) Hôtel des Voyageurs	53-54-21-29
24300	Javerlhac (north west) Auberge des Tilleuls	53-56-30-12
24630	Jumilhac-le-Grand (east) Hôtel Boueiradour	53-52-50-47
24570	Lardin-St-Lazare (south east) Hôtel de la Poste, Av. Haupinot	53-51-27-52
24340	Monsec (south west) HR Beauséjour	53-60-92-45

		Tel.
24270	Payzac (east north east nr. Lanouailles) Hôtel des Voyageurs	53-52-70-10
24370	Peyrillac et Millac (east) Auberge Deux Ecureuils	53-29-72-22
24360	Piegut-Pluviers (north) Hôtel Dauphin	53-56-41-67
24360	Piegut-Pluviers Hôtel Pelissier, 36 Rue la Libération	53-56-40-30
24800	Thiviers (east) Hôtel des Voyageurs, Rue P. Semard	53-55-09-66
24800	St Jory de Chalais (east) Auberge St Georges	53-52-04-25
24360	St Estèphe (north) Hôtel de L'Etang	53-56-82-01
24470	St Saud (east) Hôtel le Sully	53-56-97-70

● The Lot along the river Dordogne between Souillac and St Céré

46500	Alvignac Hôtel du Château	65-33-60-14
46500	Alvignac Auberge Madeleine	65-33-61-47
46130	Bretenoux Hôtel de la Source	65-38-40-02
46110	Carennac Hôtel Fénelon	65-38-67-67
46110	Carennac Hôtel des Touristes	65-38-47-07
46170	Castelnau-Montratier Hôtel des Arcades	65-21-95-52
46350	Combroux-Masclat HR Chez Crouzil	65-37-61-01
46600	Creysse Auberge de l'Isle	65-32-22-01
46600	Cuzance (nr Martel) Hôtel Barre	65-37-84-17
46600	Gluges La Bonne Friture	65-37-33-50
	Gourdon (see text)	
46200	Lachapelle-Auzac Maure Bellevue	65-37-82-32
46200	Lacave Hôtel des Grottes	65-37-87-06
46500	Miers Hôtel du Centre	65-33-63-61
46600	Martel Hôtel du Lion d'Or	65-38-52-38
46130	Puybrun Hôtel des Touristes	65-37-30-16
46500	Padirac Padirac Hôtel	65-33-64-23
46500	Padirac Hôtel du Quercy	65-33-64-68
	Rocamadour (See text)	
46170	St Paul de Loubressac la Grange du Levat	65-21-93-16
46170	St Paul de Loubressac Relais de la Madeleine	65-21-98-08

		Tel.
46200	Pinsac Hôtel du Centre	65-37-86-88
	Saint Céré (See text)	
46200	Saint Sozy Hôtel Grangier	65-32-20-14
46200	Saint Sozy Hôtel de la Renaissance	65-32-20-13
46110	Vayrac Hôtel Le Modern	65-32-50-53

Finding a gîte

Gîtes are flats, apartments, houses, villas, farm-barns etc. which can be rented for a minimum of a week. They are let fully furnished with instructions not only how to *'faire le ménage et la cuisine'*, but also on how to get the best out of the countryside. There are 300 gîtes in the Dordogne, and for a cost of 30 francs you can be sent a booklet containing all the gîtes by the Relais Departmental des Gîtes de France Dordogne-Périgord, 16 Rue Wilson, 24009 Périgueux, tel. 53-53-44-35. Most *gîtes* are in the countryside in or near a hamlet or village.

The costs are quoted per week and each *gîte* can sleep from four to 10 adults. I can give you some examples bearing in mind that high season (July/August) is about 30% more expensive than June or September. A rental completely out of season is still cheaper.

● Marquay (Ref. 907) has a three star *Gîte* for five or six adults and three children, central heating and four bedrooms. Facilities include tennis 1 km, river or swimming pool 10 km, nearest shops 3 km, doctor, chemist, SNCF 12 km away. High season 2,015 francs, low season 1,680 francs, and out of season 1,455 francs.

● Peyrignac (Ref. 146) has a two star renovated old house sleeping eight people, with three bedrooms and central heating. Facilities include fishing 4 km, horseriding and swimming pool 10 km away. High season 950 francs, low seasons 750 francs, and out of season 670 francs.

● Agonac (Ref. 261) has a one star house, shared with the proprietor, for four people with two bedrooms. Facilities, many, with Agonac 4 km, Périgueux and Sorges both 10 km away. High season 1,030 francs, low season 840 francs, and out of season 615 francs.

Many UK tour companies offer *gîte* holidays in the Dordogne and bookings and payment can be made therefore in the UK in sterling.

Chambres d'hôtes

These are the equivalent of bed and breakfast places with the evening meal negotiable *'en famille'* with the proprietor's family. Great fun but the more French language you know the more you will enjoy your stay. There are 40 *chambres d'hôtes* in the Dordogne. Prices are remarkably consistent, in the range of 120 francs to 175 francs per head for bed and breakfast, or for a couple, 170-235 francs. As in a hotel there is no minimum or maximum stay.

Holiday villages

These are smart little modern villas, usually clustered around a lake, and there are generally good local restaurants or inns nearby. For example, the village of Lapeyre near St Barthelemy de Bussière (pop 300) north of Nontron, where four or six people can stay comfortably for 1500-1700 francs per week in high season, 1000-1200 francs low season, and 800-1000 francs out of season. Another holiday village is at Clairvivre, Salagnac (pop. 1100) 10 km north east of Hautefort. The villas are quoted for three, five or six people per week, at roughly the same prices. The holiday village of 'Les Fontaines', at Milhac de Nontron is by a lake of 28 hectares (70 acres) surrounded by trees. 'La Perdicie' at Jumilhac le Grand (25 km east of Nontron); the 'Relax-super Relax' village at St Crepin Carlucet (10 km north east of Sarlat); a small village at Saint-Estèphe (5 km north of Nontron); another at Loubejac (5 km south of Ville Franche-du-Périgord); and for canoeing enthusiasts a small holiday village at Tremolat on the river Dordogne, with swimming pools and tennis. Children can stay in a *Roulotte* caravan (without horse).

Camping and caravan sites

The French take their camp and caravanning sites very seriously. Annual inspections are always made including spot checks. The facilities are always good. The sites are kept free of litter. The showers **do** have hot water. The electricity does work. Above all the management are always on their best behaviour and take pride in their site. Many are run by the local municipality with equal efficiency to their commercial counterparts. Some of the extra facilities should be checked beforehand. For instance, facilities for fishing (*pêche*), riding (*club hippique*), canoeing (*canotage*), tennis, sailing (*bateaux*), pedaloes for kids on a safe lake, cycle hire and games (*jeux*) may be available. If the campsite does not have a restaurant or café on site then there will be one in the nearest village one or two km away. Four star sites have a private swimming pool, even if near a river, as well as tennis courts and a restaurant.

The Dordogne and parts of the Lot are very popular with UK campers and caravanners. I have listed all the campsites by area and coded them as follows: RE for restaurant or café and SW for swimming lake, *étang*, *piscine* or river. The star coding relates to comfort and prices. Recent charges in the Lot have been as follows, based usually on a family of two adults and two children, per day.

Rating		Francs
x	one star	23–45
xx	two star	23–72
xxx	three star	34–81
xxxx	four star	63–132

Opening and closing dates vary considerably: a few stay open all the year. Always make a reservation in advance. If you are planning a trip in mid-summer contact the site about six weeks before you are due to go to avoid any disappointment. I have divided the region into six subsections for easy reference.

RE = Restaurant
SW = Swimming

Post code	Town/Village	Name	Tel.	Category	
24360	Busserolles	Camping Mun.	53-60-53-04	xx	RE SW
24361	Piégut-Pluviers	Les Garennes	53-56-40-22	x	
24360	Saint Estèphe	Le Grand Etang	53-56-80-93	xx	RE SW
24300	Abjat Champs-Roman	Camp. du Moulin de Masfrolet		xx	RE SW
24450	La Coquille	Le Périgord Vert	53-52-85-77	x	RE SW
24630	Jumilhac-le-Grand	La Chatonnière	53-52-57-36	xx	SW
24300	Nontron	Masviconteaux	53-56-02-04	xx	in town SW
24340	St Sulpice-de-Mareuil	Corneuil	53-60-37-66	x	SW
24340	Mareuil-sur-Belle	Le Vieux Moulin	53-60-99-80	xx	
24340	Vieux Mareuil	L'Etang Bleu	53-60-92-70	xxx	RE SW
24470	Milhac de-Nontron	Les Fontaines	53-56-71-96	xxx	RE SW
24800	Sarrazac	La Lavatre	53-62-52-06	x	
24270	Angoisse	Rouffiac en Périgord	53-52-68-79	xxx	RE SW
24270	Payzac-de-Lanouaille	Le Moulin	53-52-76-81	x	
24160	Excideuil	Le Pont Rouge	53-62-95-37	x	RE SW
24310	Brantôme	Peyrelevade	53-05-75-24	xx	in town SW
24310	Valeuil	Bas Meynaud	53-05-72-11	x	
24310	Bourdeilles	Fonseigneur Sud	53-03-73-13	x	in town SW
24350	Lisle	Le Pont	53-04-50-02	xx	SW
24350	Tocane-St-Apré	Le Pre Sec	53-90-40-60	xx	SW
24600	Riberac	La Dronne	53-90-03-10	xx	RE SW
24410	La Jemaye	Le Grand Etang	53-90-18-51	x	RE SW

Post code	Town/Village	Name	Tel.	Category	
24410	St Vincent-Jalmoutiers	Petit Moucard	53-91-71-08	xx	
24410	St Aulaye	L'Astier	53-98-54-28	xx	snacks SW
24410	Parcoul	Le Paradou	53-01-42-78	xxx	RE SW
24490	La Roche-Chalais	Les Gerbes	53-91-40-65	xx	SW

2. The next region is Périgord Blanc in the centre which includes Périgueux and Mussidan. Note that Trelissac, Boulonac, and Atur are very close to Périgueux.

Post code	Town/Village	Name	Tel.	Category	
24420	Savignac-les-Eglises	Du Moulin	53-05-00-54	xx	RE SW
24420	Sarliac-sur-l'isle	Le Nordoc	53-06-03-61	x	RE
24390	Tourtoirac	Les Rochers	Mairie	x	
24640	Le Change	La Chapelle Auberoche	53-06-04-19	x	
24640	Cubjac	L'Ilot	53-05-30-21	x	SW
24000	Trelissac	Les Garennes	53-54-45-88	xx	in town SW
24000	Boulazac	Barnabé-Plage	53-53-41-45	xx	snacks SW
24750	Atur	Le Grand Dague	53-04-21-01	xxx	RE SW
24110	Saint-Astier	Le Pontet	53-54-14-22	xxxx	RE SW
24110	Saint-Aquiln	L'Etang des Garennes	53-54-17-89	xx	RE SW
24410	Echourgnac	Les Chaumes	53-80-36-56	x	
24190	Neuvic sur l'Isle	Neuviçois	53-81-50-77	xxx	SW
24400	Mussidan	Le Port	53-81-20-09	x	RE SW
24700	Montpon-Ménéstrol	Municipal	53-80-30-98	x	RE
24700	St Geraud-de-Corps	Domaine Chanleau	Mairie	x	

Post code	Town/Village	Name	Tel.		Category
24380	St Amand-de-Vergt	Lac de Neufont	53-54-93-90	xx	SW
24330	Ladouze	Etang de la Prade	53-06-74-59	x	RE SW
24330	Ladouze	La Laurre	53-06-74-00	xx	RE SW
24260	St Felix-de-Reilhac	Le Roc de Lavandre	53-03-23-47	xx	RE SW

3. Périgueux Pourpre is the third region based on Bergerac, bisected by the river Dordogne in the south west of the department.

Post code	Town/Village	Name	Tel.		Category
24100	Villamblard	La Fontaine Rose	53-81-91-87	xx	RE SW
24140	Douville	Orphéo-Negro	53-82-96-58	xxx	RE SW
24140	Pont-Saint-Mamet	Lestaubière	53-82-98-15	xxx	RE SW
24110	Campsegret	du Bourg	53-24-22-36	xx	RE SW
24700	St Rèmy-sur-Lidoire	La Tuilière	53-82-47-29	xxx	café SW
24610	Carsac-de-Gurson	Le lac de Gurson	53-80-77-57	xx	RE SW
24130	Montfauçon	Etang de Bazange	53-24-64-79	xx	RE SW
24230	St Seurin-de-Prats	La Plage	53-58-61-07	xxxx	RE SW
24230	St Antoine-de-Breuilh		53-24-82-80	xx	RE SW
24130	Gardonne	Parc Servois	53-27-84-83	x	café SW
24520	Mouleydier	La Gravière	53-23-22-38	xx	SW
24150	Sauveboeuf (Lalinde)	Le Parc	53-61-02-30	x	SW
24150	Mauzac	Camp. du Bourg	53-22-50-57	x	RE SW
24150	Lalinde	Le Moulin de la Guillou	53-61-02-91	xx	SW
24150	Couze St Front	Maury Bas	53-61-03-07	xx	café SW

Post code	Town/Village	Name	Tel.	Category	
24100	Bergerac	La Pelouse	53-57-06-67	xx	town SW
24440	Beaumont du Périgord	Les Remparts	53-22-40-86	xxx	RE SW
24440	Naussannes	Le Couderc	53-22-40-40	x	RE SW
24240	Sigoulès-Pomport	La Gardonnette	53-58-81-94	xx	RE SW
24560	Issigeac	Le Bourg	53-58-70-32	x	café SW
24500	Eymet	Le Chemin de la Sole	53-23-80-28	x	RE SW
24540	Gaugeac-Monpazier	Le Moulin de David	53-22-65-25	xxxx	RE SW
24540	Marsalès	Vérone	53-22-62-22	xx	café SW
24540	Biron	Etang du Moulinal	53-71-61-97	xxx	RE SW
24550	Villefranche-du-Périgord	Les Terrasses	53-29-91-44	xx	SW

For instance, the three star camping at Biron has a capacity for 390 'campeurs', is open 1st April to 30th September, and the owners M. & Mme Pawlak charge for a weekend for a caravan from 250 francs (three people) to 350 francs (six people) and have three seasonal rates (Bas, Moyenne, Haute saison – 600, 700, 1,460 francs for a car and caravan with three people).

4. Périgord Noir in the south east around Sarlat with the rivers Vézère and Dordogne is the final region in the Dordogne department (from north to south).

Post code	Town/Village	Name	Tel.	Category	
24390	Nailhac-Hautefort	Le Beaulieu	53-50-46-55	x	café SW
24210	Thenon	Jarry Carrey	53-05-20-78	xx	café SW

Post code	Town/Village	Name	Tel.	Category		
24210	Fossemagne	du Manoire	53-04-43-46	xx		SW
24120	Terrasson	La Vergne	53-50-02-81	xx		SW
24290	Montignac	Le Bleufond	53-51-83-95	xx		SW
24580	Rouffignac	Cantegral	53-05-48-30	xxx	RE	SW
24120	La Cassagne-Coly	La Grande Prade	53-51-68-22	xx		SW
24290	Thonac	La Castillanderie	53-50-76-79	x	RE	SW
24580	Plazac	Le Lac	53-50-75-86	xxx	café	SW
24290	La Chapelle Aubareil	La Fage	53-50-79-23	xx	RE	SW
24290	St Léon-sur-Vézère	Le Paradis	53-50-72-64	xxxx	RE	SW
24590	Saint-Geniès	La Bouquerie	53-28-98-22	xxxx	RE	SW
24200	Marcillac-St-Quentin	Les Tailladis	53-59-10-95	xxx	RE	SW
24200	Marcillac-St-Quentin	La Veyssière	53-59-10-84	x		
24590	Salignac-Eyvigues	La Draille	53-28-93-21	xx	RE	SW
24590	Salignac-Eyvigues	Le Temps de Vivre	53-28-93-21	xx	café	SW
24370	Rouffillac-de-Carlux	Ombrages de la Dordogne	53-29-70-24	xx	café	SW
24200	Proissans/Sarlat	Le Val d'Ussel	53-59-28-73	xxxx	RE	SW
24620	Tursac	La Ferme du Pelou	53-06-98-17	x	café	SW
24620	Tursac	Le Vézère Perigord	53-06-96-31	xxxx	café	SW
24620	Tursac	Bouyssou	53-06-98-08	x		
24620	Tursac	Le Pigeonnier	53-06-96-90	xx	RE	SW
24260	Le Bugue	Le Port	53-07-24-60	xx	town	SW
24260	Le Bugue	Le Rocher de la Granelle	53-06-24-32	x	RE	SW

Post code	Town/Village	Name	Tel.	Category	
24510	Pezuls	la Foret	53-61-71-69	xx	RE SW
24510	Tremolat	Centre Nautique	53-22-81-18	xxxx village SW	
24620	Les Eyzies	La Rivière	53-06-97-14	xx	RE SW
24620	Les Eyzies	Le Pech Denisson	53-06-95-84	xx	café SW
24620	Les Eyzies	Le Mas de Sireuil	53-29-68-06	xxx	RE SW
24200	St André-d'Allas	Le Moulin du Roch	53-59-20-27	xxxx	RE SW
24200	St André-d'Allas	Villeneuve	53-59-68-06	xxx	SW
24200	Ste-Nathalène	Grottes de Roffy	53-59-15-61	xxxx	RE SW
24200	Ste-Nathalène	La Palombière	53-59-42-34	xxxx	RE SW
24200	Ste-Nathalène	Maillac	53-59-22-12	xxx	RE SW
24370	Prats de Carlux	La Chataigneraie	53-59-03-61	xx	café SW
24370	Cazoules	La Borgne	53-29-81-64	xx	
24370	Peyrillac et Millac	La Combe de Lafon	53-29-72-36	xx	RE SW
24370	St Julien de Lampon	Le Bourniou	53-29-83-39	xx	RE SW
24370	St Julien de Lampon	Le Mondou	53-29-71-50	xx	RE SW
24370	Calviac	Les Chenes Verts	53-59-21-07	xxx	RE SW
24200	Sarlat	Les Perrières	53-59-05-84	xxxx	SW
24200	Sarlat	Caminal	53-59-37-16	x	RE 1½ km
24200	Sarlat	Le Val d'Ussel	53-59-28-73	xxxx	RE SW
24200	Sarlat	des Bories	53-28-15-67	xx	RE SW
24220	St. Cyprien	Le Garit	53-29-20-56	xxx	SW
24480	Allès	Port de Limeuil	53-22-02-10	xx	RE SW
24220	Le Coux	La Faval	53-31-60-44	xxxx	café SW

Post code	Town/Village	Name	Tel.	Category
24220	Le Coux	Le Clou	53-31-63-32	xxx RE SW
24220	Beynac	Le Capeyron	53-29-50-03	xx
24200	Carsac-Aillac	Aqua Viva	53-59-21-09	xxx RE SW
24200	Carsac-Aillac	Le Rocher de la Cave	53-28-15-67	xxx café SW
24250	Grolejac	Le Granges	53-28-11-15	xxxx café SW
24220	Vitrac	Le Clos Bernard	53-28-33-44	xx café
24220	Vitrac	Soleil Plage	53-28-33-33	xxx RE SW
24220	Vitrac	La Bousse de Caudon	53-28-33-05	xx café SW
24220	Vezac	La Cabane	53-29-52-28	x
24220	Vezac	Les Magnanas	53-59-51-79	xx RE SW
24220	Vezac	La Plage	53-29-50-83	xx SW
24220	Vezac	Les Deux Vallées	53-29-53-55	xxx RE SW
24250	La Roque-Gageac	La Butte	53-28-30-28	xxxx RE SW
24250	La Roque-Gageac	Beau Rivage	53-28-32-05	xxx RE SW
24250	La Roque-Gageac	Le Lauzier	53-29-54-59	xxx RE
24250	La Roque-Gageac	Verte-Rive	53-28-30-04	xx
24250	Castelnaud	Maison Neuve	53-29-51-29	xx SW
24170	Siorac	Le Port	53-31-63-81	xxx SW
24480	Le Buisson de Cadouin	Pont de Vicq	53-22-01-73	xx 1 km SW
24480	Cadouin		53-22-02-73	x RE 500m
24170	Belvès	Le Moulin de la Pique	53-29-01-15	xxxx RE SW
24170	Ste Foy-de-Belvès	Les Hauts de Ratebont	53-29-02-10	xxxx RE SW
24250	Cénac-St-Julien	Le Pech de Caumont	53-28-21-63	xxx SW

Post code	Town/Village	Name	Tel.	Category
24250	Cénac-St-Julien	Cénac Plage	53-28-31-91	x
24250	St Cybranet	Bel Ombrage	53-28-34-14	xxx RE 4km
24250	St Cybranet	Cascades de Lauzel	53-28-32-26	xx SW
24250	St Cybranet	Le Céou	53-28-32-12	xxx RE SW
24250	Daglan	Moulin de Paulhine	53-28-20-88	xx café SW
24250	Daglan	Le Peyrugue	53-28-40-26	x café SW
24170	St-Pompon	Le Trel	53-28-43-78	xx SW
24170	Domme	Le Perpetuum	53-28-35-18	x SW
24170	Domme	La Croix des Près	53-28-35-92	xx café
24170	Domme	Le Bosquet	53-28-37-39	xx
24250	St Martial-de-Nabirat	Le Carbonnier	53-28-42-53	xxx RE SW

5. Further to the east as the river Dordogne (Michelin Map 75) meanders into the Lot department, there are camping-caravan sites which should be considered. From west to east they are as follows:

46200	Lanzac	du Pont	65-37-02-58	xx RE village
46200	Souillac	La Paille Basse	65-37-85-48	xxxx RE SW
46200	Souillac	Les Ondines	65-37-86-44	xx RE town
46200	Pinsac	Verte Rive	65-37-85-96	xxxx RE village
46200	Pinsac	Port de Pinsac	65-32-64-00	xx RE
46200	Lacave	La Rivière	65-37-86-02	xxx RE SW

Post code	Town/Village	Name	Tel.	Category
46200	Meyronne	La Plage	65-32-23-26	xx SW
46200	St Sozy	Les Borgnes	65-32-21-48	x café SW
46200	Mayrac	Le Pit	65-32-25-04	xxx RE SW
46600	Creysse	Du Port	65-32-20-40	xx RE river
46110	Carennac	Les Prés Nabots	65-38-55-42	xx village
46130	Tauriac	Municipal	65-38-62-46	x
46130	Puybrun	La Sole	65-38-52-37	xxx café SW
46130	Bretenoux	La Bourgnatelle	65-38-44-07	xxRE/SW village
46400	Saint-Céré	Soulhol	65-38-12-37	xxxRE/SW town
46600	Gluges (nr Martel)	La Gabarre	65-37-33-70	xxx river
46200	Salignac	La Draille	65-28-90-31	xxx river
46110	Vayrac	Les Granges	65-32-46-58	xxx river
46110	Vayrac	La Palanquière	65-32-43-67	xx river
46110	Vayrac	La Peupleraie	65-32-40-80	x river

6. Hinterland

Post code	Town/Village	Name	Tel.	Category
46500	Alvignac	Municipal	65-33-60-83	xx
46500	Gourdon	Les Segalières	65-38-70-41	xxx
46130	Loubressac	La Garrigue	65-38-34-88	xxx
46530	Loupiac	Les Hirondelles	65-37-64-34	xx
46600	Martel (N of Dordogne)	Les Falaises	65-37-33-59	xxx

Post code	Town/Village	Name	Tel.	Category
46600	Martel (N of Dordogne)	La Callopie	65-37-30-03	x
46500	Padirac	Des Chênes	65-33-65-54	xxx
46500	Mayrinhac-Lentour	La Cascade	65-38-14-01	xx
46350	Payrac	Le Panoramic	65-37-98-45	xx
46350	Payrac	Le Picouty	65-37-95-05	xx
46500	Rocamadour	Les Tilleuls	65-33-64-66	xxx
46500	Rocamadour	La Fajadou	65-33-67-48	xx
46500	Rocamadour	Le Relais du Campeur	65-33-63-28	xx
46300	Rouffilhac	Le Pech	65-41-19-95	x

CHAPTER FIVE:
BLACK DIAMONDS, WALNUTS AND RURAL FARE

The Dordogne is a land of milk and honey! The range of delicious food products locally grown must rank almost as high as anywhere in the world — nearly in the same league as Burgundy. The 50,000 farms in the region stock 175,000 sheep, 120,000 pigs and many thousands of geese and ducks.

Digging for diamonds

One major speciality is the famous 'black diamond' of Périgord and Quercy. This curious, woody, earthy *'goût de terroir'* truffle, thinly sliced, seasons patés, sauces, soups, stuffings, omelettes, even joints. It is often blended with the local foie gras and poultry. It flavours the turkey meat *'ballotines'* and also cold galantines in aspic. Each year the price per kilo of the black truffle increases as restauranteurs in France and elsewhere vie with each other to buy this rare object at over £300 per kilo (£80 + per pound). Under oak trees known as *'chênes truffières'* on the roots about a foot underground, grow mysteriously round, black, pungent fungi, shaped like a squash ball — the truffle of Périgord. Only about one oak tree in a thousand has these sought-after growths, but nevertheless a few tons are found each year. When we lived in the neighbouring Lot (Quercy) department we owned three *'chênes truffières'*. Each winter when we were not living on our modest estate the local farmer would seek them out with truffle-pig or truffle-hound on a lead and we would receive small tins enclosing 'black diamonds'. Just what proportion of his finds he sent to us we will never know, but doubtless it was very small.

Watching the female pig or hound in search of the elusive treasure is, to the Anglo-Saxon, immensely funny! The animal, carefully trained by its owner, digs and scratches away until within a few inches of the find, when the greedy beast is hauled away, just in time, and given an alternative reward. The truffle season is from November to March. The overall supply is in decline, perhaps only 10-20 tons a year — it depends on rain in mid summer — and many efforts have been made to create truffle 'fields' by seeding artificially. Our local farmer tried and failed most ignominiously.

I have tracked down 50 villages in the Dordogne where truffles are currently found in commercial quantities. These include Thiviers, Excideuil, Thenon and Terrasson. Sorges, 20 km northeast of Périgueux is one of the most important centres. Coly, 25 km north of Sarlat, has a *'truffière-pilote'* scheme to grow the black diamonds commercially which has put the local truffle hounds out of business! Brantôme, in the north of the department, has a *'foire des truffes'* over the Christmas period. Bergerac, in the west, has a number of truffle-growing villages such as Faux. If you want to try truffle dishes, you can pick from *'à la cadurcienne'* (with saffron, *'en croute'* (with bacon and foie gras wrapped in crisp pastry) and *'sous les cendres'* (wrapped in pork slices and cooked in hot ashes).

Nutty choice

The Dordogne is the second largest single area in the world growing walnuts. About 5-7,000 tons are harvested each year. The Romans introduced the 'Juglans Regia' walnut variety, named after Jove/Jupiter, in the fourth century. Walnut oil for cooking is a local speciality and the nuts are to be found in a variety of dishes. We owned some walnut trees but the squirrels and field mice always seemed to get there first! Brantôme has a *'foire aux noix'* in October, but Doissat, southwest of Domme, claims to have *'la noyeraie la plus importante d'Europe'*. Manzac-sur-Vern, southwest of Périgueux, also produces walnut oil. Altogether about 50 villages including Riberac and Montignac produce walnut crops and the trees are often to be found on the road verges to make collection easier. Saint Sulpice d'Excideuil near Thiviers has an old-fashioned windmill for crushing nuts.

The walnuts ripen in late July and August. Theoretically large canvas sheets are spread under the trees to catch the nuts, which must be collected before the soft green skins harden and blacken. The early 'wet walnuts' are then served as part of a salad or hors d'oeuvre. In Périgord there are still stone oil mills where the nuts are crushed to extract the valuable walnut oil, after being dried over kilns. A green salad with rich walnut oil is a favourite delicacy.

Most markets in the Dordogne will offer you piles of nuts — for immediate eating or for cooking. Varieties include the Franquette (in new plantations), the Corne (which grows on the chalky hillsides), the Marbot (which we grew in the Lot) and the popular Grand Jean grown around Sarlat and Gourdon. My wife always spends a small fortune on rich walnut cakes made by the *'grandes pâtisseries'* in Périgord and Quercy. It requires great self control not to eat them before we get back to England.

Mushroom magic

Twelve varieties of mushrooms and *cèpes* are to be found all over the Dordogne, particularly around Bergerac and Chancelade. The *'girolle'*, variety has a pink and subtle flavour. Villefranche du Périgord in the southeast corner has marvellous cèpes markets. The size will often reach a foot in diameter. These huge flat-topped fleshy mushrooms are a great delicacy. *'Cèpes à la périgourdine'* is cooked with bacon, parsley, garlic and verjus (juice from unripe grapes). *'Daube'*, a beef stew, is enlivened with cèpes. *'Omelettes aux cèpes'* are often seen on local menus, particularly in and around Périgueux.

Foie gras

Foie gras is the enlarged liver of goose or duck that has been force-fed on maize. However unpalatable this sounds it is big business in Périgord and hundreds of small farmers produce this delicacy, served hot, or cold in slices, or made into a paté. They are seasonally fresh in winter from November to February and are then tinned for consumption during the rest of the year. *Confit de canard, d'oie, de porc* or *de dinde* are pieces of duck, goose, pork or turkey salted, then cooked and preserved in their own fat in earthenware jars.

Brantôme has a 'foire du foie gras' in mid winter. Sainte-Alvère halfway between Sarlat and Bergerac has a commercial foie gras factory, as does Eymet in the southwest corner. On the approaches south of Périgueux you can see half a dozen *foie gras* farmers offering their produce at roadside shops. Pure goose fat is used as an alternative to walnut oil or butter in Périgord cooking.

Cheese choice

Although the Périgord cheeses are not the finest in France there are half a dozen regional varieties, mainly differing goat's cheeses. From Cubjac east of Périgueux comes Cujassou goats cheese. Échourgnac southwest of Riberac produces 'le trappiste' made by the local trappist monks. Other villages and towns noted for their cheeses are Borrèze, Carves, Journiac, Marsac sur l'Isle, Saint Anthoine d'Auberive, St Georges Blancaneix and Thiviers. Some people like a mature goats' cheese, maybe two years old, others like it best when very creamy-fresh and perhaps a few weeks old.

Game to eat

Sangliers or wild boar are another rare speciality, and they are now reared, but roam fairly freely at Cantillac, Montignac, La Roche-Chalais, St Felix and St André de Double. Some of these villages also rear *cerfs* (deer), *chevreuils* (roe-deer) and *faisans* (pheasants). Goat-like animals called *caprins* are reared at Coulaures, Vergt de Biron and Vieux Mareuil, and *gibier* (game) at Faniac, Coursac, and St Martin de Riberac.

Sweet moments

The honey is particularly good at Tamnies and St Maime de Peyerol. Your favourite patisserie or croissants will probably have come from Bussière-Badil, Nontron or St Avit-Senieur. Lamothe-Montravel produces a special patisserie called *'croquembouches'*. Meyrais, west of Sarlat, makes officially *'le meilleur pain de France'* baked over wood fires and sold in *tourtes* (literally tarts) of 4½ kilos each. Ideal for very hungry children!

Fruits of the sea

With so many large peaceful rivers traversing the Dordogne it will be no surprise to see fish on the menu. *'Carpe à la Neuvic'* stuffed with truffles and *foie gras* is one delicious dish, another is *'fricassée de volaille aux écrevisses'* which is chicken and crayfish in cream and white wine sauce. Salmon from Mouleydier, *truites* (trout) from Lequillac de l'Auche and *'poissons d'eau douce'* from La Coquille are all worth their place on the menu. Expect to find and taste eels, lampreys, pike, barbel and morels. Commercial fisheries (*pisciculture*) are to be found at Cours de Pile, Dagla, La Force, Fouleix and Manzac sur Vern.

Fruity favourites

There are many fruits to be found in the department. Église Neuve de Vergt, south of Périgueux, is the regional strawberry commercial centre. There is a co-op at Vergt which specialises in the berries. You can expect to see apples, plums and grapes *'sur la table'* in the summer and autumn. There are also cherries and pears from Eyliac just east of Périgueux.

Regional specialities

Although the Dordogne produces good quality wines, cider is to be found at Jumilhac le Grand and Mazeyrolles. The local mineral source waters are bottled at Queyssac (called Corail), at Castels (called Font-Chaude) and also at St Martin de Gurçon and St Pierre de Frugie. Excideuil has a notable *'herboristerie'*, a herbal centre. Sarlat has many unusual delicacies. Liqueurs made of the cream of walnuts and of *genièvre* (juniper berries), as well as *foie gras*, walnut oil and, believe it or not, *'les pommes de terre sarladaises'*. Ultra-special spuds baked and truffled! Comberande-et-Epeluche near Riberac has a large flour mill which welcomes all visitors. There are a score of large villages which have a complete range of local grown/reared specialities from *foie gras* to walnuts, *cèpes* to freshwater fish. Visit little Villamblard, or Villefranche du Périgord, which have regular produce markets with all the delicacies I have mentioned.

Food fairs

Varaignes is noted for its turkey fair. Their *'foire aux dindons'* dates from the time of Henri IV. For nearly four centuries the *'dindons'* have been shepherded *'à pied'* for 5 km in a ritual procession! Domme has two specialities, *'ris de veau aux morilles* and *'ragoût d'écrevisses'*. Douzillac has an annual onion fair, whilst Issigeac produces *'souris vegetales riches en vitamine C'* which is named 'Actinidia de Chine'.

On the menu

Even the simplest, humblest little café-restaurant will have a smashing *'plat du jour'* for about 25 francs. Possibly a *'cassoulet à la périgourdine'* of sausages, bits of pork and white haricot beans plus whatever titbits including goose the chef has decided **that day** to add! *Sobronade* is a thick stew-soup, first cousin to cassoulet but including onions, carrots, turnips, leeks, celery, and spiced with herbs and garlic sprinkled over the ham, pork and white beans. The ubiquitous chicken turns up as *'poulet rouilleuse'* in a rich white wine and garlic sauce, thickened with chicken blood. *'Dodines de volaille'* (boned marinated chicken, stuffed and braised) is another popular dish. *'Tourtière'* is chicken and salsify pie.

Rabbit (*lapin*) and hare (*lièvre*) also appear frequently. *'Lièvre à la royale'* is probably one of the best dishes to be found in central France. A rich truffled sauce is served over a hare boned, stuffed with veal and bacon, and marinated in wine **and** brandy! *'Ballotine de liévre à la périgourdine'* is the same but different! The hare itself is stuffed with foie gras, truffles, rabbit and pork or veal and flavoured with brandy.

Duck (*canard*) is a staple and appears in many forms. As *'alicuit'* stewed giblets with mushrooms, beans and garlic; as *'magret'* it is the breast this time, boned and fried or grilled; as *'cou farçi'* it is the neck, now stuffed with *foie gras*, minced pork and truffles. *'Pintade'* is the name for guinea fowl, which comes stuffed with truffles and *flambéed* with brandy sauce.

Peasant-style soups include *'bougras'* which is vegetable soup − at least six different vegetables − with *'boudin'* (black pudding) stock. *'Tourin'* is onion soup with egg yolks, tomatoes and a gratin of goat cheese. *'Tourain'* is a white garlic soup with eggs and goose fat. *'Chabrol'* is the name for the local custom of drinking red wine mixed with soup dregs! *'Chou farçi'* is a whole cabbage cooked in white wine stuffed with mushrooms, veal and pork and simmered for a long time.

Various fritters are made called *'merveille'*, *'gougnette'*, *'jacque'* (a kind of apple pancake) or *'roussette'*. *'Cajasse sarladaise'* is a rum-flavoured cake or pastry to have at the end of the meal, or perhaps *'millas'*, a maize flour cake sprinkled with sugar as a pudding. Perhaps the richest dish of all is *'tourte de truffes à la périgourdine'*, an incredible tart with foie gras and sliced truffles sprinkled with brandy!

Gourmet holidays

Special gourmet holidays in Périgord are organised by the main departmental tourist office in Périgueux. There are ten large villages where these *'stages de cuisine périgourdine'* take place — usually in the October — April period. In the north at Vaunac, Negronde (near Thiviers), Sorges and Eyliac, in the centre at La Jemmaye, Lamonzie-Montastruc, and in the south at Les Lèches, St Crépin-Carlucet, Baneuil and Meyrals.

There are four varieties of holiday. (1) Three day weekend at a farm, or (2) at a two star hotel in Sorges. The tarif of 600-900 francs per person includes *'pension complète'* where the intricacies of the Périgord cuisine are taught you in a practical sense. (3) a week at a farm-gîte for 700 francs, and (4) another weekend course for 790 francs in a two star hotel which also includes a visit to a *'truffière'* as well as full pension. A warning though, that a visit to a goose farm is not for the squeamish!

Some of the confit dishes you will learn to prepare include *'foie gras entier au naturel'*, *'paté de foie'*, *'confits'* (eventually preserved and tinned), *'cou farçi'* (stuffed goose necks), *'confit aux pommes sautées'*, *'confit en salade'*, *'garbure'* (vegetable soup with many herbs, dried ham and goose pieces), *'ragouts'*, *'bouillis'*, *'coeurs en sauce'*, *'magret en cocotte'*, *'coeurs poêlés'*, *'foie poche'*, etc. The Monbazillac wine producers naturally recommend that their chilled white wine should always be served with *foie gras* — they are probably right!

The Monbazillac collection

The local wine growers have inspired some delicate recipes. From Monbazillac come the following:

Grapefruit with Monbazillac (Léon)

Slice a pink grapefruit in half, cut the flesh out, add Monbazillac and serve chilled in a small melon.

Cantaloupe with Monbazillac (Le Relais de Gabillou)

Open a cantaloupe and remove the seeds. Fill with a glass of Monbazillac, a dash of Angostura bitters and a few walnut halves. Serve chilled on crushed ice.

Trout Monbazillac (Le Relais de Gabillou)

Place trout on a bed of minced shallots in a buttered dish. Cover with chopped mushrooms and 3 dl. of Monbazillac and cook in oven. When done, remove the trout and keep warm. Reduce the sauce by half with crème fraiche, thickening with butter and flour. Pour over trout and serve hot.

Fresh Salmon Monbazillac (Hôtel de Bordeaux, in Bergerac)

Cover the salmon fillet with a layer of chopped mushrooms, a layer of tomatoes and another layer of mushrooms. Butter a Pyrex dish, sprinkle with minced shallots, add a glass of Monbazillac. Put the salmon fillet in the dish and cover with buttered aluminum foil. Bring to a boil, then put in oven for 10 minutes. Keep fish warm and reduce the sauce, adding crème fraiche. Stir until thick. Strain and pour over salmon.

Gratin d'écrevisses au Monbazillac (Restaurant Le Cyrano, in Bergerac)

Shell the shrimp (10 per person) and simmer in a spicy court-bouillon. Sauté 100 gm. of shallots, 300 gm. of diced carrots in a pan. Add crushed shrimp shells and 2 dl. of Monbazillac, cook 35 min. Strain and reduce by two thirds. Add 50gm. of crême fraiche and reduce by one third. Add 35 gm. of sliced butter. Cook spinach separately. Pour sauce over spinach and cooked shrimp. Sprinkle with bread crumbs au gratin.

Monbazillac is the perfect companion for any dessert. Serve it with ice cream, sherbet, custards and pastry. Add it to fruit salad, or crêpe batter (Mr. Lestang of Eymet recommends substituting Monbazillac for water: 50% milk, 50% Monbazillac).

Here are three simple but sweet ideas:

Pruneaux au Monbazillac (Relais de Gabillou)

Bring 1 kg of dried prunes to a boil in 1 litre of Monbazillac with 2 cl. of Grand Marnier and 1 clove. Cool in refrigerator for 12 hours and serve chilled.

Fresh Raspberries or Strawberries Monbazillac (Léon)

Select ripe, undamaged berries and rinse carefully. Place in parfait glasses, sprinkle with 1 teaspoon of sugar and 5 cl of Monbazillac.

Sherbet for 10 (La Flambée)

1 bottle Monbazillac
250 gm. sugar
250 gm. mixed fruit with juice (e.g. apricots and peaches)
Follow instructions on your ice cream maker.

Not to be outdone, eleven two or three star local hoteliers (all regrettably well over a prix fixe of 50 francs) have produced a wide range of dishes where it is absolutely 'indispensable' that they are cooked with the red wines of Pecharmont. I list a few of them and hope the reader has the appropriate resources!

Le filet de brochet braisé au Pécharmont
Le civet de truites au Pécharmont
Les aiguillettes de boeuf au Pécharmont
Le ris de veau braisé au Pécharmont

La truite saumonée au Pécharmont
L'escalope de foie de canard poêlé à l'infusion d'enchalot-
tes et au vin de Pécharmont
Medaillon de cou d'oie farci du Périgord avec sa sauce au
Pécharmont et sa couronne de pâté fraiches
Tournedos nouveau accompagné d'un Pécharmont
Le baron de laperau au Pécharmont
Le civet de lamproie au vin de Pécharmont
Le foie gras aux reinettes au Pécharmont

Fish ending

Finally, whilst writing about local recipes, I was impressed by
the excellent *'poissonière'* by the covered market in Périgueux
whose fish is handed to the customer in a pink wrapper with
four recipes written on it − *'dorade au four'* − *'rougets aux
champignone'* − *'lisettes moutarde'* − and *'limandes à la
bretonne'*. Clever merchandising that!

If you want a fishing holiday (with guaranteed freshwater
trout included) contact Association 'Sur le pas de Jacquou Le
Croquant', 3 Rue Elisée Reclus, 24210 Thenon, tel.
53-05-21-06 (NW of Montignac). They also offer a weekend
'Foie Gras − cuisine gastronomie'. Both at the same price of
1560 francs per person.

CHAPTER SIX:
HISTORICAL BRIEFING

The department is the richest in France, perhaps in the world, for its mementoes of the Palaeolithic era, the chipped stone age, when Neanderthal man lived in 'cluzeaux' or troglodyte caves. Skeletons of the type of man who lived on earth 150,000 years ago were discovered at Le Moustier in 1909, and at La Ferrassie in 1909-1911. The Dordogne is classified as **the** capital of prehistory and this subject is covered more fully in Chapter Thirteen with details of the extraordinary paintings, engravings and rock drawings on view to the visitor. Dolmens, tumuli and menhirs show curious basic religious symbols.

Roman occupation

Before the Romans arrived the main local tribe were the Celtish Bellovagues (around Belvès), the Ligurians and the Petrocorii (around Périgueux). In the heavily wooded massif between the rivers Vézère and Corrèze to the east lived the Druids who fiercely resisted the Roman legions under General Crassus. In the four centuries of their occupation the Pax Romana brought relative prosperity to the region, Emperor Augustus' reign was particularly beneficial. Aqueducts from this time can still be seen at Carsac-Aillac, (Moulin Neuf), Boulazac, Calès, and St Laurent-sur-Manoire (Vesone). Mosaics can be viewed at Port Sainte-Foy-et-Ponchapt and Cénac-et-St Julien, which also has a *hypocauste* and canals. Roman villas can be seen at Coursac, Bussière, Bergerac (Bracarius) and Lussas. Montcaret in the southwest corner was a prosperous Roman town in the first and second centuries with mosaics, hypocauste, baths, villa and flour mill (Nodin). Nontron was the site of a Roman 'castrum', and Villetoureix has the Roman tower called 'La Rigale'.

Toscane took its name from its Tuscan rulers, and Jaure from the Roman word Jove for Jupiter. Manzac-sur-Vera took its name from the Roman Manitius, and Riberac from the Latin Ribeira or river. Marcillac-Saint Quentin was named after the Roman villa there of St Quentin. Roman coins were found at La Chapelle-Aubareil and Colombier. A Roman river port was sited at Badefols, and L'Isle has a Roman bridge.

In Périgueux, built by the Romans in the first century and then known as Vesuna, there is still a tower of that name and amphitheatre which holds 20,000 spectators, a Roman villa, the Pompeia (Rue des Bouquets) and parts of the original town ramparts. Overall in the Dordogne there are 800 churches of which 400 are Romanesque and 100 are truly Roman, fundamentally from the first and second centuries.

Arrival of Christianity

Despite the worship of Jove and Vesuna by the Romans, Christianity came to Périgord in the fourth century. Sainte Foy (AD 303), St Hilaire and St Just were early martyrs in the fourth century, followed by St Front in the fifth, St Cybard and St Aquiln in the sixth, St Astier, St Pardoux, St Avit, St Amand de Coly in the seventh and St Sacerdos in the ninth century. St Front was the most famous, born at Lanquais, a brave miracle-worker to whom the cathedral of Périgueux is dedicated. St Martial and the mysterious St Amador were important early evangelists.

After the fall of Rome the dark ages descended again. There were invasions by the Allemans who destroyed Périgueux and left behind a large village of the same name north of Riberac; by the Visogoths in AD 407, beaten by Clovis at Poitiers in AD 507: the Saracens in AD 711, crushed by Charles Martel at Poitiers; the Normans who devastated Brantôme, Paunat, Périgueux and Saint Astier in AD 849; the English in the Hundred Years War — and so on.

The Christian church survived, almost flourished. Certainly the Emperor Charlemagne was a great benefactor, sponsoring Benedictine churches or abbeys at Sarlat, Brantôme (AD 786) and Périgueux. The Benedictines, Dominicans, Cistercians, Augustinians and the Knights Templars founded religious orders in the twelfth century all over the Périgord. Their abbeys, priories and churches can still be seen.

Pilgrims path

From the tenth century onwards for seven hundred years, the pilgrims (known as Jacobites or Coquillards) wending their way on foot towards Saint-Jacques of Compostella in north-west Spain, passed through the Dordogne. The routes were clearly identified with hospices and chapels en route. From Limoges there were two main pilgrim roads. To Firbeix, La Coquille (the cockle shell was the pilgrim emblem), Thiviers, Sorges, Les Piles, Chancelade (west of Périgueux) towards Saint Foy la Grande. Some pilgrims went through Périgueux south to Chalagnac, Douville, Pont St Mamet, Bergerac, Issigeac, and Eymet towards La Réole. The eastern route came through St Yriex, Lanouaille, Excideuil, St Raphael, Ajat, Rouffignac, Le Bugue, Cadouin (a pilgrim abbey), to St Avit-Senieur and Marmande. The pilgrims usually passed through or started their pilgrimages, which might take a year, at Vézelay in Burgundy, inspired by the monks of Cluny.

The religious Albigensian crusade percolated west from Albi to the Dordogne. In AD 1147 the abbot of Sarlat invited the famous St Bernard to preach there against the 'new' Albigensian faith which continued for another eighty years until it was brutally stamped out by the Anglo-Norman Simon de Montfort in AD 1209-1229.

The English connection

The marriage in AD 1154 between Henry Plantagenet, the future King Henry II, to the divorced Queen Eleanor of France was a significant date. The beautiful young woman was heiress to the region of Aquitaine which included Périgord. However, intermittent skirmishes and minor battles started very quickly. Richard Coeur de Lion succeeded to the throne in 1189. At his coronation in London one of my ancestors, William de Force, was one of his four banner-bearing friends. Richard was more French than English and spent most of his time in Aquitaine hunting, fighting and holding court.

Périgord produced a quiverful of the romantic ballad-singers, the troubadors. one of them, Bertran de Born, was a personal friend of the king's as well as being a swashbuckling freebooter. Bertran was born at the château of Born near Salagnac, but spent most of his life in the great château of Hautefort. He retired to Saint Trie and became a Cistercian monk. Three other well-known local troubadours were Barnard de Ventadour, who was buried at Boisseuilh with Bertran de Born, Guillaume de la Tour, who lived near Sainte-Nathalène, and Arnaud de Mareil, who was born at the château of that name in AD 1150. Arnaut Daniel was born c. 1150 at the château of Riberac. Their songs of unrequited love and romance were sung for 70 years at all the local courts in France. Elias Carels was born at Sarlat in 1190 and dedicated his lyrics to every noble he could, including an emperor and a king. René Lavaud in 1912 wrote a book entitled 'Les Trois Troubadours de Sarlat', and Dante Alighieri and Petrarach wrote movingly of the Périgordan troubadours.

The Knights Templars established themselves at Sergeac, between les Eyzies and Montignac. Their influence in Périgord was considerable and they owned many properties including Jumilhac-le-Grand, Allemans, Angoisse, La Cassagne, Saint Naivent and many others. Cherveix-Cubas, Comberanche-et-Épeluche and La Dornac were Templar preceptories. Condat-sur-Vézère was a Templar commanderie. These soldier-knights became so prosperous and the Popes and the French Kings grew so jealous that in AD 1312 the order was abolished and all of their possessions confiscated. In Domme you can see graffiti on the prison walls written by the wretched Templar prisoners.

Battle scars

At the Treaty of Paris in AD 1259 Périgord was ceded by the French King St Louis to England. Many bastide towns were then built, mainly by the English. These were new commercial ventures, with a right to have their own market-place, frequently on a major road or near a river.

The towns were built in a rectangular defensive grid shape with strong walls. The fortified church would overlook the main arcaded square. I have located over 50 towns and villages involved in the savage fighting including the bastides of Beaumont, Beauregard et Bassac, Eymet, La Bastide, Molières, Monestier, Saint-Aulaye, Sainte Foy la Grande, Saint Louis en l'Isle, Vergt and Villefranche de Lonchat. The two earliest were Lalinde and Villefranche du Périgord built about 1259-1261. The three finest survivors are Monpazier, Domme and Beaumont. King Edward II was particularly keen on encouraging the building of bastides.

The Hundred Years War started in AD 1337 and the Périgord suffered as badly as any other are. Domme was one of the first battlefields in AD 1347. The first cannon were used by the French in AD 1339 besieging the Château Puyguilhem near Thenac. The Black Prince pillaged 500 villages in Périgord and Quercy and it is remembered to this day!

There were many magnificent feudal castles established by the tribal chieftains overlooking key river crossing points or dominating small towns. If you are interested in these matters I would recommend a visit including Beynac et Cazenac, Biron, Bourdeilles, Castelnaud-la-Chapelle, Excideuil, the Château de Tayac at Les Eyzies, Jumilhac-le-Grand, Lanquis, Mareuil, Piégut-Pluviers (partly destroyed by Coeur de Lion in AD 1199), the Château de la Marthonie at St Jean-de-Côle, the Château de Fénêlon at Sainte-Mondane, Château de Salignac-Eyvignes, Château de Losse at Thomac, and Château de Puyghuilhem at Villars. Lamothe-Montravel is the **actual** site of the battle of Castillon where Sir John Talbot and the English army were destroyed in 1453.

In the Middle Ages there were four great baronies in Périgord, the Bourdeilles (north west), Mareuil (north west), Beynac (on the Dordogne) and Biron (south east).

During 1373-7 the French general Du Guesclin reconquered much of Périgord, but after Agincourt the region became English-owned again.

Feuds and plague

By the end of the fifteenth century, with the departure of the English, prosperity slowly returned, until in 1594 there started a local peasant uprising, the revolt of the Croquants. Towns affected were St Martial, Milhac, Grun, Creyssansac and Grignols. Finally when their wretched leader, Buffarot, was broken on the wheel in AD 1637 in the market place of Monpazier, the revolt fizzled out.

As if this was not enough outbreaks of plague decimated the population and savage religious wars between the Catholics and the Protestants (called Huguenots) broke out in 1550. The first Protestant martyr was burnt at the stake at Sainte Foy la Grande in 1542. The Dordogne, and particularly Bergerac and La Force, were Protestant centres. Pitched battles were fought in many villages and towns. Three years after the slaughter of the Huguenots on St Bartholomew's Day in 1572, when 10,000 Huguenots were killed (including a Delaforce family), three times that number emigrated, mainly to Holland and the UK.

The Revocation of the Edict of Nantes at the end of the seventeenth century brought temporary peace. That is if you exclude the damage done by the Fronde rebellion of 1653. At the end of the seventeenth century there were three designated 'capital' towns in Périgord — Périgueux (pop. now 35,000), Bergerac (pop. now 28,000) and Sarlat (pop. now 10,000).

Château Montfort near Vitrac was a refuge for Huguenots and stands high above the river Dordogne near Turnac, and should be visited. In 1574 Sarlat was burned and pillaged by the Huguenots. In 1575 the Huguenots captured Périgueux disguised as peasants coming to market and vandalised shrines and churches.

Revolutionary zeal

The French Revolution brought no comfort to Périgord (the region was called the Dordogne in 1798). A leading 'citoyen' Lakanal caused many fine aristocratic and ecclesiastical buildings to be torn down in the name of 'fraternité'. Anything, and anybody, connected with the old regime was at risk.

Seventy priests in Périgueux were guillotined and Sainte-Alvère was burned. The Dominican Convent of Saint Pardou-la-Rivière was closed down, as was the important Benedictine abbey of Fontgauffier at Sagelat. Boschaud and Chancelade were destroyed. The château at Montignac was turned into a stone quarry by the new libertarians! The châteaux at Jayac, Mareuil, and at La Force were burned or destroyed in 1790.

War and resistance

The Dordogne lost a high proportion of their young men 'morts pour la patrie' in World War I when the population of nearly one million was reduced to 400,000. Thirty years later it became one of the chief resistance centres in World War II. In 1941 the first English paratroops jumped with weapons for the resistance movement at Beleymas 25 km southwest of Périgueux. The local monument is called *'stèle de Lagudal'*. The Wehrmacht destroyed a number of villages including St Martin de Fressengens, Saint Vincent-le-Paluel, Saint-Germain-et-Mons, Mouleydier, Rouffignac, St Cernin-de-Reillac and Pressignac-Vicq. The bastide at Lalinde was also destroyed by the retreating Nazis in 1944.

At Saint Germain-des-Près there is a monument to the English parachutists who died in action at la Moranchie fighting alongside the Resistance members. Mussidan was one of the very few towns in France to be awarded the Croix de Guerre after their liberation in 1944 for Resistance activities during the war. The camp de Virole at the hamlet of Saint-Etienne-de-Puycorbier has a monument commemorating the Maquis activities in the region. At Vergt-de-Biron on the third Sunday in May there is a commemoration to remember those deported to Germany during World War II. The famous Resistance group called 'Bir-Hakeim' was based in the Dordogne; eventually its survivors were publicly shot. Members of the RAF still visit the Dordogne to keep up with their (ageing) *maquisard* friends. The Entente Cordiale continues to work harmoniously at times!

Scribblers' birthplace

Henry Miller called the Dordogne the 'cradle of the poets'.

Besides the many troubadours of the thirteenth century, Pierre de Bourdeille, known in the literary world as Brantôme, was a soldier of fortune who guarded Mary Queen of Scots imprisoned at Leith. In later life, a crippled abbot of Brantôme, he wrote *Ladies of Love* and *Lives of Famous Men and Great Commanders*. An eccentric notorious character of the sixteenth century, the abbot was a contemporary of Michel Eyquem de Montaigne, who lived near Bergerac. Montaigne was a gourmet philosophical essayist with several '*bons mots*' to his credit. '*Que sais-je?* (What do I know?), which is now the title for a widely marketed range of French general knowledge books. '*Il faut être toujours botté et prêt à partir*' (One should always be booted and spurred and ready to leave).

Étienne de la Boetie, Montaigne's great friend, who translated the Greeks Plutarch and Xenophon, wrote fine sonnets and was a native of Sarlat. Another well-known 'Dordonigne' was the late seventeenth century Archbishop la Mothe-Fénèlon, who wrote the controversial work '*Télémaque*', which a century later was a '*succès fou*'. Eugene Le Roy was a well-known nineteenth century novelist of the Dordogne and wrote 'Jacquou le Croquant' about the sufferings of the French peasantry. The Dordogne's best known character is, or was, the long-nosed Cyrano de Bergerac, who appeared in Edmond Rostand's play of 1897. He was a swordsman, a poet who loved the lovely Roxanne, who eventually returned his love despite his abnormality.

Other notables

In the mid nineteenth century Pierre Magne, a government minister from Périgord, encouraged railway systems which brought prosperity until phylloxera decimated the vineyards. The Dordogne produced no famous marshals or politicians, although the Talleyrand-Périgord was a notable family. Minor generals of note included Fournier-Sarlavèze, born in Sarlat in 1773, Daumesnil, born at Périgueux in 1776, and, in the nineteenth century, Général Bugeaud, who pacified Algeria.

Dutch links

You will see many Dutch visitors and settlers in the Dordogne.

They have strong links, as we do, with this charming, warm countryside. They sheltered as many refugee Huguenots in the sixteenth and seventeenth centuries as came to Britain. Bergerac wines were shipped to London and Bristol, and Monbazillac sweet white wines went to the Netherlands — and still do. Now there are almost as many Dutch resident in the area as there are British. The latter are said to own up to 3000 second or main homes, which is why I have included a chapter on house purchase in this book.

In the twentieth century one of the growth industries is that of tourism. The many sights — man-made and natural — can be explored from little hotels, or *gîtes*, or camping sites scattered over the department. *Dordogne on a Budget* locates and lists them for your enjoyment. The main local tourist offices are also shown, where you will meet every courtesy (although it helps if you can speak some French!)

Some famous citizens

● Generals

Two of Napoleon's favourites came from the region: Pierre Daumesnil born 1776 in Périgueux, fought in Egypt and lost a leg at Wagram. Fournier-Sarlovèle was born in Sarlat in 1773 and fought in Spain and Russia. Général Bugeaud was born in Exideuil and pacified Algeria in the nineteenth century. He was helped by Marshal Canrobert of St Céré, who distinguished himself in the Franco-Prussian War of 1870.

● Philosophers

Cyrano de Bergerac was a seventeenth century philosopher of the Bergerac region. Edmond Rostand 'borrowed' his name for his nineteenth century play. Joseph Joubert (1754-1824), author of 'Pensées' came from Montignac. Maine de Biran, born 1766 in Bergerac, was another noted philosopher. Michel de Montaigne (1533-97) lived in western Dordogne in the château of that name.

● Rebel

Buffarot, the weaver from Capdrot, led the Croquants and was brutally executed at Monpazier in 1637.

73

● Religious fanatics

Geoffroi de Vivans, the Huguenot leader, stormed Domme and Sarlat in the late sixteenth century.

● Writers

Eugène le Roy (1836-1907), author of 'Jacquou le Croquant' set in L'Herm castle and the region, decribes the doomed sixteenth century peasant revolts. Francoise Maynard (1582-1646) lived in St Céré and wrote sonnets, odes and letters. Pierre de Bourdeille (1535-1614) wrote as 'Brantôme' of court gossip, and biographies of the military. Etienne de la Boetie (1530-63) of Sarlat, friend of Montaigne, wrote radical political works. François de Salignac de la Mothe-Fénélon (1631-1715) wrote 'Télémaque' at Carennac.

● Troubadors

Bertrand de Born, Giraut de Borneil, Aimeric de Sarlat and Bertrand de Gourdon wrote and sang their romantic verses in the twelfth century in the Courts of Love sponsored by kings and lesser nobles.

● Historian/mathematician

Jean Tarde (1561-1638), born at La Roque-Gageac, was also an astronomer and cartographer.

● Painter/Cartoonist

Jean Lurcat, born 1892, who lived in St Céré, turned tapestry-making into an art form.

● Eccentric

Antoine Orélie de Tourens (1825-78) of Tourtoirac, was the self-appointed king of Patagonia and Araucania.

Part Two:
Regional Tours

CHAPTER SEVEN:
THE GRAND TOUR

For visitors with a week or ten days in which to see the best
of the Dordogne I have devised an attractive '**Grand Tour**'
based on the following interests:

(1) The prehistoric wonders of the Vézère valley

(2) The fabulous castles mainly sited along the river Dordogne

(3) The English-French bastide towns surviving from the
Hundred Years War

(4) The best of the romanesque abbeys and churches (including Rocamadour)

(5) The wine regions of Bergerac and Monbazillac

I have interspersed them with visits to the main towns of
Périgueux, Bergerac, Sarlat and Nontron, including a wander
through the neighbouring Lot following the river Dordogne.
If this sounds too tiring, you might prefer to spend say, three
days each in the main towns using them as a base for daily
excursions. Most visitors will arrive by car from the north either
on the N21 from Limoges or the D539 from Angoulême. As
all the towns are covered more fully in the regional chapters
I am listing the route with brief notes on each place, perhaps
with a hotel recommendation.

Nontron (pop. 4000) on the B675 on a hill with narrow
winding streets overlooking the valley of the river Bandiat, is
not particularly distinguished. It has a twelfth century tower,
ramparts and a noted doll and toy museum. You can eat well
on the typical '*confits du Périgord*', *pâtisseries*, game and river
trout. The Grand Hotel Pelisson in the town centre has a 54
franc menu and makes a good base from which to see the
northern sites of Green Périgord including Jumilhac-le-Grand,

La Coquille, Mareuil-sur-Belle, Varaignes and Bussière-Badol.

Head south on the D675 to **Brantôme** (pop. 2100), an elegant small town famous for Pierre de Bourdeille, a scandalous warrior, poet, court gallant and chronicler of the sixteenth century. The Dronne and its tributaries bisect the town, and Charlemagne's abbey and four tiered clock tower are notable sights. There are many good restaurants, and the hotel at 8 Place Charles de Gaulle run by the Versaveau family, tel. 53-05-71-42 is good value, with easy parking. Brantôme is a good base to see the châteaux of Bourdeilles, Richemond and Puyguilhem.

Then go southwest to **Riberac** (pop. 4300) by the D710 along the valley of the Dronne via Lisle and Tocane St Apre. The mundane little town claims to be the capital of *'Périgord blanc'* (wrong, Périgueux is) and it is in fact the number one equal town in the Green Périgord. It is a mystery to me why the region is so popular with the English and Dutch. The Hôtel de France, Rue M. Dufraisse, tel. 53-90-00-61 is reasonable value.

Due south to **Mussidan** (pop. 3300) via the D709 through wooded countryside which hides to the east the châteaux of Segonzac and Le Bellet on the way. Twinned with Woodbridge, near Ipswich, Mussidan, once a Huguenot centre, has little to commend it except for its folklore museum André-Voulgre. Hotel-Restaurant des Voyageurs, 40 Rue de la Libération, tel. 53-81-00-12 offers value.

Southeast on the D703 through the Forest du Landais to **Bergerac** (pop. 28,000), the second town in the Dordogne. For many years we used to drive rather idly through the town centre but in the last few years the city fathers have restored the old town to much of its former dignity. It is the tobacco centre of France and has a museum to prove it. It is also the centre of the Bergerac, Pécharmont and Monbazilac wine area with a wine museum and excellent wine co-op to prove that also. Several one star hotels include Le Provence, 2 Place Clairat, tel. 53-57-12-88, and Hotel Le Pozzi, near the Préfecture, tel. 53-57-04-68. Bergerac makes an excellent base from which to visit the vineyards and Montaigne's château 40 km west.

Southeast of Bergerac, south of the river Dordogne is *bastide* country including Eymet, Beaumont, Monpazier and Villefranche-du-Perigord. I recommend a visit to one or more, and Monpazier in my view is the most interesting. I would chose **Eymet** (pop. 3000) as a base because it is becoming popular with English settlers. On the D935 south of Bergerac there are two stops, at Monbazillac to see the château and taste the wines in the manor house, and also to see the château of Bridoire 6 km southwest. Eymet has a battered fourteenth century keep, and a *bastide* central square with arcades. The Hôtel Beauséjour on Boulevard National, tel. 53-23-81-35 offers good value with menus about 50 francs.

From Eymet go eastwards by minor roads following the river Dropt to **Issigeac** (pop. 700) where the town hall was the former Bishop of Sarlat's château. A few kms east is the handsome but private fifteenth century Château de Bardou (walk down the driveway to see the outside). Keep on cross-country to **Monpazier** (pop. 600), a classic English-built thirteenth century *bastide* and centre of the Croquant peasant revolt 1594-1637. The central *'place'* with its arcades and fortified church is a delight. As a pivotal place for the Anglo-French battles of the fourteenth and fifteenth centuries it is appropriate that the two hotels are called 'de Londres', tel. 53-22-60-64, two star but no restaurant, and 'de France', 21 Rue St Jacques, tel. 53-22-60-06, one star but with a good restaurant. From Monpazier, the great château of Biron standing on a major outcrop 8 kms south is in my view a must, as is the bastide town of **Villefranche du Perigord** (pop. 800) further east overlooking the river Lemance.

Northeast via the D53 to **Belvès** (pop. 1700), a medieval village perched on a hill just west of the D710. There are many old houses, a belfry and covered market. Try the Hotel de France, 1 Avenue Paul-Crampel, tel. 53-29-11-80.

Siorac-en-Perigord (pop. 900) is 7 km north on the D710 and overlooks the river Dordogne, indeed has its own *'plage'* or beach for canoes-kayaks. The château, mainly seventeenth century, was originally built by the English. The four hotels here are rather expensive, Le Trefle à Quatre Feuilles, tel. 53-31-60-26 being the most reasonable. **Cadouin**, 11 km west is an essential visit to see abbey and cloisters.

Having arrived at the great river Dordogne let's take stock. To the west lie a dozen fine castles in the 40 km stretch heading for Bergerac. To the east for 60 kms towards Souillac lie a score of slightly more glamorous châteaux, including Berbiguières, Les Milandes, Fayrac, Beynac, Castelnaud, Montfort and Fénélon. To the north lies Le Bugue and the prehistory valley of the Vézère leading northeast to Montignac. My own recommendation would be to go to Sarlat (or one of the outlying village/towns such as Domme or La Roque-Gageac) and spend five days visiting 'Castleland' and 'Prehistoryland' in comfort and style.

From Siorac then either go north to **Le Bugue** (pop. 2800) via **Le Buisson** on the D25 to Les Eyzies (pop. 900) and view the many grottos and then east on the D47 to Sarlat or follow the river road D703 on the north bank of the river via **St Cyprien** (pop. 1800) to **Beynac et Cazenac** where you should definitely stop off and climb (or drive) up the hill to see the strong, aggressive fortress once captured by Richard Coeur de Lion. alternately held by the British then the French, then the British again. This dominating castle has been skilfully repaired and is very photogenic. Half a dozen other castles can be seen from the summit. The quiet little Hôtel-Restaurant de la Poste, Les Terrasses, tel. 53-29-50-22 is a good bet (but closed in winter).

Keep on the D703 to **La Roque-Gageac** (pop. 400), one of the most attractive riverside villages in France. The contrast between the steep grey rockface, old tiled roof houses and the wide blue-brown-grey river is remarkable. The three two star hotels are quite expensive. Cross the river at **Cénac** (pop. 900) which lies at the foot of **Domme** (pop 1000) which has 180° views of the river valley from its summit. This medieval *bastide* town with its own deep grottos, cliff walks, covered market and gardens is well worth a visit. Try the Hotel Lou Cardil, Grande Rue, tel. 53-28-38-92, or Nouvel Hotel, Place de la Halle, tel. 53-28-38-67.

Across the river via **Vitrac** (pop. 650) which has three relatively expensive hotels, north on the D46 to **Sarlat-la-Canéda** (pop. 11,000). In my view this is the most attractive town in the Dordogne. Bisected by the D704 heading north towards Brive, it is a gem. Visit the catherdral, Masion de la

Boetie, and wander round the superbly restored old squares, narrow streets and in particular the old hotels (town mansions) of Plamon, Maleville, Gisson and Grezel. The tourist office has predictably occupied one of the most attractive town houses. The curious twelfth century Lantern of the Dead, 50 metres east of the cathedral, the sixteenth century courts of justice, Goose Market Square, Rue des Consuls and other pretty squares, some with fountains, make half a day's perfect visit (out of season). Le Moulin du Roi is an elegant restaurant tucked away in a golden niche, as is the restaurant Gueule et Gosier in the Rue de la Samandrie — both with good fixed price menus. The Plâce de la Liberté is the main square. Henry Miller called Sarlat 'Paradis des Français'. Several modest one star hotels include Les Recollets, 4 Rue J. J. Rousseau, tel. 53-59-00-49 and the Lion d'Or, 48 Avenue Gambetta, tel. 53-59-00-83. Sarlat is ideal for local visits to prehistory grottos and the châteaux of Puymartin, Commarque, St Crepin, Salignac and Le Claud.

From Sarlat the Grand Tour takes you southeast into the department of the Lot, initially south on the D704 leaving Montfort castle on the west for 30 km to **Gourdon** (pop. 5000). This medieval town, encircled by a tree-lined boulevard, has a number of thirteenth century narrow streets with names like Zig-Zag, La Bastidette, and Tortue, a sixteenth century chapel and hôtel de ville. The views from its summit of the river valleys of the Bleou, Ceou, Melve and La Marcillande are superb. It is a useful base from which you can explore parts of Quercy and Périgord and there are several tourist circuits. The splendid wall-paintings in the caves of Cougnac, about 2 km northwest, are nearly as famous as Lascaux. Try the Hôtel 'Les Routiers', La Madeleine, tel. 65-41-02-63 on the eastern outskirts of town, or the Hotel Terminus, Avenue de la Gare, with swimming pool, tel. 65-41-03-29 also on the east side near the station.

South on the N20 to **Payrac** and then east on the winding D673 takes one to **Rocamadour**, one of the most spectacular sights in France. After Lourdes, Rocamadour ranks as the pilgrim site of France. The identity of the twelfth century St Amadour is rather vague, but miracles from that date brought Henry Plantagenet, king of England, and numerous French

79

Kings to be cured here. There are a cluster of churches, basilica, crypts and chapels clinging to the 500 metre high cliffs reached by paths and steps. The musician Poulenc has a Museum-Treasury dedicated to him, and at the top of the hill is a fourteenth century fortress. Look too for Roland's sword, Durandel, sticking out of the cliff face, for the set of bizarre frescoes, at the ninth century black church bell, the 14 stations of the cross, and nerve yourself to climb the 223 steps of the Via Sancta. Rocamadour (pop. 800) is a pilgrimage centre with many hotels at the foot of the cliffs and at the top at L'Hospitalet I noticed several restaurants offering reasonable prix fixe menus, including the Hôtel Sainte-Marie and Hôtel des Voyageurs. Parking is easiest at the summit near the fortress. Nearby are separate sanctuaries for butterflies, barbary apes and eagles.

Next northeast via the D673 to **Alvignac** which has the quiet Hôtel-Restaurant du Château, tel. 65-33-60-14. Nearby is a small thermal spa. Then on to **Padirac**, a village made famous for its incredible 'Gouffre'. Reached by lifts and steps underground you can take a boat trip around three of the 23 kilometres of subterranean lagoons between Padirac and **Montvalent** amphitheatre in the Dordogne valley. Look for the Devil's Hole, an enclosed 100 metre circle (with an emergency green crane for hauling out survivors?) round the gaping chasm. The lagoons have curious names including *'pas du crocodile'*, *'lac de la fin'* and *'lac du découragement'*, There is also a Tropicorama Zoo where you can see exotic birds and monkeys. Both *'Chasm'* and zoo are closed in winter until Easter. There are several small hotels including du Quercy, tel. 65-33-64-68 and Padirac, tel. 65-33-64-23, and restaurants. It is best to avoid the months of July-August unless you are a glutton for crowds.

From Padirac east on the D673 to see the Grotto of Presque, the sweet little château of Montal and the town of **St Céré** (pop. 4300) in the valley of the river Bave, overlooked by the towers of St Laurent. St Céré is an attractive little town full of charm and history with fifteenth to seventeenth century houses, squares and streets. A good place in which to stay to explore the countryside of the northwest Lot. Look at the

Hotel du Parc, tel. 65-38-17-29 or Hotel de la Truite Dorée, tel. 65-38-17-54. The 'Mon Auberge' and 'Le Tromp l'Oeuil' restaurants offer good four course meals for about 55 francs. The river runs through the centre of the town and local fish are often on the menu.

Head northwest on the D940 and then a minor road D19 in the Bave valley for 12 km to the massive fortress of **Castelnau** which has the title *'2ème forteresse de France'*. (Not to be confused with Castelnaud which glares across the Dordogne at Beynac.) Once the garrison in the eleventh century powerful red-stoned castle numbered nearly 2000. An essential visit.

Follow the D30 road alongside the Dordogne to **Carennac** (pop. 400) which ranks as one of the three prettiest villages in the region. Here you will find the old priory where the author, Fénélon lived, many sixteenth century houses, a castle, and a fortified gateway. Try the Auberge du Vieux Quercy, tel. 65-38-69-00 or Hotel-Restaurant Fénélon, tel. 65-38-67-62. Off the beaten track but definitely worth a visit.

Now continue along the D43 parallel to the river Dordogne through **Creysse** (chateau) and St Sozy, to the famous Grottes de Lacave, where an electric train shuttles one for nearly 2 km underground looking at lakes, reflections and stalactites. Marvellous for children of all ages. For many years we took our English friends to visit Lacave on our own tour. The Hôtel des Grottes, tel. 65-37-87-06 is reasonable.

Keep on the D43 past the Château du Belcastel on a white craggy outcrop and then to the Château de la Treyne, a fourteenth to seventeenth century building now a hotel, towards **Souillac** (pop. 4000) which has an abbey, well restored, deriving from the tenth century. The English twice occupied the town in the Hundred Years War. It used to be a convenient stopping place for us and we have breakfasted at most of Souillac's hotels. This is a favourite summer resort for English visitors, with many campsites, grottos and castles within easy reach. Try the Hôtel de la Cascade, Rue de Timbergues, tel. 65-37-84-49 or Hôtel-Restaurant Le Beffroi, 6 Place St Martin, tel. 65-37-80-33.

From Souillac take the D15 north back from the Lot into

the Dordogne, then the D62 through Borreze to **Salignac-Eyvignes** (pop. 1000), a medieval fortress still belonging to the same family, open to the public.

Now west on the D60 past the Château St Crepin, on to the familiar D704. There are two alternatives now. Westwards cross country via **Marquay** and the river valley of the Beune towards Les Eyzies and join the D706 north up the valley of the Vézère to our target which is Montignac. On the way there are superb grottos, troglodyte villages in the cliffs, several minor châteaux, and the pretty village of St Léon-sur-Vézère which ranks amongst the three prettiest in the Dordogne. A simple classic twelfth century Benedictine priory, and by the river a perfect Dornford Yates château for which I would give my eye-teeth! Alternatively take the easier but less interesting main road i.e. the D704 past the château of La Filolie into **Montignac** (pop. 3200) whose fame is known due to the discovery of Lascaux caves. The chapter on prehistory gives appropriate information. Sadly you now see a superb replica of the original, called Lascaux II, as man's heavy breathing was literally destroying the original famous wall and rock paintings. Montignac has excellent picnic facilities beside the river bridge. A pleasant town with a good folklore museum named after Eugene le Roy, the writer of Jacquou le Croquant (the local peasant revolt). There are three modest hotels in Montignac, La Grotte, tel. 53-51-80-48, Le Lascaux, tel. 53-51-82-81, and du Périgord, tel. 53-51-80-38, all with sensible restaurants. A good place to stay out of season.

Follow the D704 parallel to the Vézère past **Condat** and **Le Lardin**, north west on the N89 with Peyraux Château on your right to a major road junction. The road to Périgueux is 40 kms due west, but there is one more final *'circuit'* with some treasures to come. So keep north on the D704 bypassing St Rabier until you see on your right the massive but elegant château of Hautefort, which is one of the finest in the Dordogne (closed December – January). An essential visit.

Keep north on the D704, branch west on the D76 to **Excideuil**, another classic château, and keep on the D76 northwest towards **Thiviers** (pop. 4200), a busy market town with truffle and *foie gras* markets and fairs, and the Château de Vaucolour. Try the Hotel-Restaurant des Voyageurs, Rue

P. Semard, tel. 53-55-09-66. Being on the N21 Thiviers is a useful base from which to see the northeast of the Dordogne including the elegant château of Jumilhac-le-Grand, and those of La Coquille, Puygyilhem, as well as Excideuil and Hautefort.

West on the D707 is **St Jean de Côle** with its château, cloister and eleventh century priory chapel. With its Gothic bridge over the river Côle and greensward, I give it — just — the accolade of being the prettiest village in the Dordogne. My publisher and I will be intrigued to learn from readers whether they concur!

The Grand Tour has now come full circle. Brantôme is 26 kms southwest and our final destination, the préfecture town of Périgueux, some 50 kms due south. The minor road D3 is more peaceful than the D939.

Périgueux (pop. 40,000) is almost dead centre of the Dordogne department, bisected by the River Isle and dominated by two grand cathedrals. Five roads feed into the town, the N89 from the southwest, N21 from the south, N89 from the southeast and the N21 again to the east. It is the major Roman site of the region with its arena, the Tower of Vesonne and villa of Pompeius. Although the old quarters near the St Front Cathedral are not in the same class as Sarlat, the city fathers have tried hard. The half dozen museums are predictably the best in the Dordogne (the Military and the Périgord in particular). The town is well worth a stay of two or three days as there are several regional circuits. There are plenty of hotels and restaurants from which to choose. Try the Hôtel-Restaurant Lion d'Or, 17 Cours Fénélon, tel. 53-53-49-03 or Hôtel-Restaurant des Charentes, 16 Rue Denis Papin, tel. 53-53-37-13.

I hope the reader will enjoy this grand tour as much as my wife and I did.

CHAPTER EIGHT:
PÉRIGUEUX AND REGIONAL TOURS

I have visited this handsome prefecture town (40,000 pop.) many times and always feel guilty. In 1575 my Huguenot forebears behaved disgracefully, ravaged most of the town, and pointlessly destroyed the tomb of St Front in the cathedral and the clock tower in the Église de la Cité. They had every reason to protest at the Catholic church's excesses but their despair turned to forming aggressive crusading armies.

One of the best views of Périgueux is from the bridge Pont des Barris that crosses the river L'Isle which in turn winds around the town. If you look across from the southeast bank the view is dominated by the huge white Byzantine cathedral of St Front, with its many unusual cupolas. This twelfth-century Romanesque building, and its cloisters, was the meeting place for hundreds of weary pilgrims on the way to Santiago de Compostella.

Périgueux is proud of its visible 2000 years of history and its Roman remains are proof of this legacy. In the first century AD the Gauls lived in the nearby hills and the Petrocores with their vigorous new masters under Emperor Hadrian built a prosperous city which they called Vesuna. It had temples, public baths, richly decorated villas with mosaics and frescoes, and an amphitheatre. The 24 metre high tower of Vesuna stands proudly in its garden near the Rue Mosaique, the Gallo-Roman wall, the Porte de Mars, Porte Normande, Rue Romaine, and the Boulevard des Arènes, which surrounds what is left of the Roman amphitheatre. The Rue du Gymnase and Rue des Gladiateurs are also links with the Roman past.

Périgueux city tour

Collect a street plan from the tourist office at 1 Avenue d'Aquitaine, tel. 53-53-10-63. You will see that the old

Roman city is clustered near the church of St Étienne de la Cité within a few minutes walk west from the tourist office. The great cathedral is about a ten-minute walk east. You head for the river through the old town, now mainly pedestrianised, with its Renaissance hotels (town mansions). Try parking in the Place Bugeaud, close to the Place de la Libération.

In addition to the Roman 'city', the St Front Cathedral and cloisters I have listed five other points of interest.

1 Try to visit the morning markets, specially on Wednesday. They are held in two small squares, the Place de la Clautre and Place du Coderc, which are both close to the covered market (Halles) with its fish shop Poissonerie Moderne.

2 The Renaissance houses, staircase and town gates in the Rue de la Sagesse, Rue Limogeanne and Rue Aubergerie (Maison des Consuls, Daumesnil, and many others).

3 Food shops in Rue Taillefer including Pierre Champion, which is full of foie gras, cheeses, truffled produce, wines of Bergerac and Monbazillac.

4 Museum of Périgord in Cours Tourny, north of St Front Cathedral, which is crammed full of prehistoric finds including Chancelade Man.

5 Military Museum in Rue des Forges. Générals Daumesnil and Bugeaud were prominent Périgordin military heroes.

The itinerary suggested by the tourist office has ten sites in the Gallo-Roman 'cité antique' and twenty clustered together in the 'vieille ville'. You should allow half a day for each itinerary. In high season there are guided tours five days a week excluding Sunday and Monday.

Restaurants change owners and chefs sadly all too often. However, judging by my own experience the following four restaurants are worth a call. Le Bordeaux, 1 Rue Wilson, had 'poulet à la Périgourdin' on its 55 franc menu when I went there. Le Vieux Pavé in the Rue de la Sagesse had 'cervelle de veau meunière' on its 58 franc menu. In the Rue Salmon we discovered the Restaurant Le Benson, with a 55 franc menu, and the Restaurant Lou Chabrol with one at 50 francs.

Modest hotels include:

Hôtel des Charentes, 16 Rue Denis Papin, tel. 53-53-37-13, and almost next door the Midi-Terminus at No 18, tel.

53-53-41-06 – both opposite the railway station. Both have restaurants. Hôtel des Voyageurs is at No 22, tel. 53-53-17-44. The station is in the northwest of town, 1 km from the tourist office and Roman city. Also try the Lion D'Or, 17 Cours Fénôlon, tel. 53-53-49-03; the Univers, 18 Cours Montaigne, tel. 53-53-34-79; or L'Oasis near the Hôtel de Préfecture (Town Hall) tel. 53-53-45-31, all with restaurants.

Périgueux has a year-long calendar of events including Carnival on Shrove Tuesday (the largest in the whole of Aquitaine), concerts, jazz (at Le Benson restaurant amongst others), Bastille Day on 14th July, song contests throughout the summer on Thursday evenings, a mime festival the first two weeks in August, ballet, theatre in the streets etc.

The modern suburbs of Chamiers, Trelissac and Boulazac are not particularly attractive, but Périgueux does make an excellent centre for touring the surrounding countryside. The tourist office has devised no less than eight such circuits, and most of them can be done by bus for about 100 francs for a whole day trip.

● **Northwest tour**
Start northwest on N139 to **Chancelade** to see the abbey founded in the twelfth century by the Augustinians. It was occupied several times by English troops in the Hundred Years War, and later damaged by the Huguenots. In the chancel is a window showing Thomas à Becket canonised in 1173. The fortified Merlande Priory on the D1 8 km northwest was built in the twelfth century by the monks of Chancelade. Raymonden was the archeological site where the prehistoric man called 'Chancelade' was discovered.

Keep on the N139 to Château-l'Evêque which is mainly fourteenth-century overlooking the river Beauronne and was owned by the Archbishops of Périgueux. Then northeast on the D3 to **Agonac** (pop. 1000) to see the mainly eleventh-century fortified church of St Martin, to Ligueux on the D74, then to **Sorges** (pop. 1000) which has two two-star hotel-restaurants, to see the Truffle Museum (closed Tuesdays).

Next southwest on the D106 to see the Château de Jaillac, to Cornille and the Château de Caussade in the Lanmary forest, a classic moated fifteenth-century fortress with square towers in each corner. Still southeast across the N21 to Éscroire and the Renaissance Château des Bories (guided tours, tel. 53-06-00-01) on the river l'Isle. Through the woods to the winding valley of Auvézère with more châteaux and Romanesque churches at Le Change and Baisilac (near the local airport) and back into Périgueux. Total mileage is around 80 to 90 km.

● **Western tour**

Heading westwards on the N139 past Chancelade to Marsac, Razac to **Annesse-et-Beaulieu** with thirteenth-century church and old 'maison de curé, and across the river Isle to St Astier, which is dull apart from a twelfth-century church and château of Puy-Ferrat (3 km northwest). Follow the river via Neuvic (fifteenth century château), Douzillac, Sourzac (pop. 1000, Grotto of Gabillou, no visits, a petrified fountain and Romanesque church) into **Mussidan** (pop. 3300). This modern town which is bisected by the river l'Isle, is twinned with Woodbridge in Suffolk. The religious wars of 1569 involved the town in four sieges which badly damaged it. In World War II the Resistance movement put up a good fight and Mussidan was awarded the Croix de Guerre with bronze star. The Saturday markets which first started in 1497 are worth a visit as is the André Voulgre Museum, Rue Raoul-Grassin (closed Tuesday). Here you can see some of the 223 prehistoric designs found at the grotto of Gabillou. The sixteenth-century Pietà in the church is worth seeing. Don't leave without trying the apéritif Lou Cacaou, made of local wine flavoured with walnut oil. It is made by Distillerie Allary tel. 53-81-00-51.

Mussidan is a possible holiday centre. Modest hotels include the Parc, 25 Avenue Montaigne, tel. 53-81-02-70; Périgord, 37 Avenue Gambetta, tel. 53-81-05-85, and Des Voyageurs, 40 Rue de la Libération, tel. 53-81-00-12. Restaurants include Le Cadran Solaire, Lou Marmitou and Le Relais de Gabillou. Besides a one-star camping site there is a municipal swimming pool, tennis, cycling and the equestrian centre of Beauperier. The Ceramic Club has 150 members with three-week summer courses at 1 Rue Villechanoux. Mussidan is also one of the best fishing centres in the region, since four rivers nearby (Beauronne, Lèches, Crempse and Grolet) produce record catches, including a 36 pound carp and 15 pound brochet. Mussidan is on the major Paris/Bordeaux/Lyon railway line which makes it a good holiday centre for people without a car.

Head northwest on the D38 to St Michel-de-Double in the centre of the forest and huge lakes, Echourgnac (Trappist convent), La Jemaye, which has a twelfth-century church and an aqua park of 21 hectares east of the D708. Then go along the D708 northeast to **Riberac** (pop. 4300), so-called capital of Périgord blanc.

The sights include the twelfth-century church of Faye, Tuesday morning and Thursday market, fishing, a riding centre called 'La Bride du Welsh' is at Madrix, tel. 53-90-03-53. Large swimming pools, a circuit of Romanesque churches (Siorac, Bourg du Bosc, Allemans and Vanxains) and a municipal camp site — these are the modest offerings to the tourist. Hotels include La Gare tel. 53-90-01-02, Univers, 2 Avenue de Verdun, tel. 53-90-04-38, Chêne Vert, 42 Rue Couleau, tel. 53-90-05-65 and Cheval Blanc, 54 Rue 26 Mars 1944, tel. 53-90-16-47.

One of the largest foies gras farmers is Les Toupines de Riberac, whose products are available at Copaldro, Place Debonnière, tel. 53-90-11-73. Also there are Anny-France, Route de Périgueux, tel. 53-90-01-44 and La Truffle du Périgord, 35 Rue du 26 Mars, tel. 53-90-00-47. The main festival takes place for three days around 23rd July each year when you can see magnificent floral floats. There are numerous fishing and bowling competitions.

Go back to Périgueux on the D709 south and southeast to **Chanterac** with its fortified Romanesque church and **Saint Aquiln** (pop. 400) which has a Romanesque-Gothic church. Tucked away in the woods are two rather fine fifteenth-century châteaux, La Martinie and du Bellet (both near Segonzac). The circuit is about 120 km and if you visit both Mussidan and Riberac it will take a full day.

● **Peasant's revolt tour**

The tour of the Pays de Jacquou le Croquant is named after the peasant's rebellion of 1594-5. The circuit is east and southeast of Périgueux and covers about 130 km. Initially go due east on the D5 south and parallel to the Auvézère river to Bassillac, Le Change (several minor châteaux and Romanesque churches), Blis-et-Born, Montagnac d'Auberoche, Brouchard, Bauzens (twelfth-century church) to Ajat. The Château of Restignac was built in 1811 – 17, burned down by the Germans in World War II and recently restored. It is a large rectangular building similar in style to the White House in Washington. Next to it is the Romanesque church – they are both worth a stop.

Southeast across the N89 takes you into **Thenon** (pop. 1500), which has the hotel-restaurant Chez Serge at Les Tournissons, tel. 53-05-20-31, with **full** pension currently at 120 francs a day. Go southeast on the D67 to Auriac, which, with its fifteenth-century chapel of St Rémy and twelfth-century fortified church, the celebrated local author Eugène le Roy put into his novel. Continue on to **Montignac** (pop. 3000) bisected prettily by the river Vézère. An excellent place on which to base a holiday for prehistory tours, and there are plenty of châteaux nearby (Talleyrand, Losse, Fanlac, Puy-Robert, La Filolie) as well as the Eugène le Roy Museum, Regourdou and Lascaux II sites. The folklore festival lasts for a week at the end of July and is one of the annual events in the Dordogne. Try the Hôtel Le Périgord, Place Tourny, tel. 53-51-80-38, in a quiet square overlooking the river, or Hôtel Restaurant de la Grotte, Rue 4 Septembre, tel. 53-51-80-48 with good menus from 48 francs, but a little noisy. The stone bridge across the Vézère dates from 1777 and bisects the small town, with the parish of St Pierre on the west bank, and St Georges on the east bank. Apart from the D704, a busy road, Montignac has a certain charm.

Travel west to Fanlac with its twelfth-century church and château, south to Thonac with the fifteenth-century Château de Losse (guided tours tel. 53-50-70-38) and twelfth-century church, and sixteenth-century Château de Belcayre to Sergeac with a Romanesque church, inland via little Saint Léon with its exquisite church and Château de Clerans on the river. Last time I was there the Judas trees were in full purple bloom and an elderly disgruntled beagle was barking. I took the riverside walk past the fairytale castle and could hear the Vézère bubbling away. It was a moment to treasure. The

Auberge du Pont and Hôtel de la Poste have 50 franc menus.

Next on to the famous site of Le Moustier, then Plazac (Roman church) and Rouffignac, which the Germans burned in 1944 but thankfully they failed to destroy the grottos and caves. Finally visit the Château de l'Herm in in the forest of Barade (guided tours, tel. 53-05-41-71, closed Wednesday). Built in 1512, the bloody historical events which took place here made it an excellent setting for Eugène le Roy's novel. On to Saint Geyrac with its twelfth century church, Les Versannes, and back on the D710 into Périgueux. Depending on how many prehistoric sites, châteaux and museums you visit, the 130 km will take between one day and one week!

● Northern tour

This northern tour takes in Chancelade, then Merlande, then keeps on the D1 to **Lisle**, which has a sixteenth-century château and twelfth-century church. The valley of the river Dronne and the D78 takes one to Bourdeilles (pop. 750). My wife and I recently climbed up to the top of the château which was founded in 1259 and owned by the English. It has lovely views of the river, water mill, rape fields and three manor houses. Look at the dungeon in the main tower. A second sixteenth-century Renaissance château with a gilded salon was built within the main castle wall. Guided tours to both cost 20 francs (closed Tuesday) and are well worth the money, tel. 53-53-85-50. The older château is free on Saturdays. The hotel-restaurant Les Tilleuls in the main square is good value.

Keep on the D78 northeast following the river to **Brantôme** (pop. 2100) beside the Devil's Anvil rock and other limestone crags. Every visitor to the Dordogne should spend a few hours here. The river Dronne encircles and bisects the little town which is dominated by the old abbey on the northern bank. The town is known as the Venice of Périgord with canals and waterwheels. The Boulanger Viennoise (opposite a huge char-cuterie in the Rue Victor Hugo) offers an intriguing selection of olive rye bread, nut raisin bread, and multi-grain bread. In the Place du Marché is a wine merchant specialising in Pércharmant wines. Near Charlemagne's abbey is the Syndicat d'Inititative in a little grey tower, and the restaurant Cave which has a good 58 franc menu. Walk across the bridge at the Quai Bertin and read General du Gaulle's stirring appeal to the French nation on the wall outside the Hôtel de Ville which is next door to the abbey building with a tall, tiered belltower, and the Museum of Prehistory. A small statue and fountain also commemorates Brantôme's first citizen, the swashbuckling poet-writer, Pierre de Brantôme. Hôtel-restaurant l'Auberge du Soir, tel. 53-05-82-93 has a good menu, but the best value hotel in my view is at 8 Place Charles de Gaulle, tel. 53-05-71-42. There are many curious megaliths and dolmens around Brantôme, indeed a classic one is **La Pierre Levée** as you come in on the D78. There is a dance festival in mid-July, and Franco-Britannique fête in early August.

Head east on the D78 and then make a little detour north to Condat-sur-Trincou, a curious little village with a twelfth-century chapel, and visit Champagnac-de-Belair, which has two hotel-restaurants; du Château, tel 53-54-80-23, and the Voyageurs, tel. 53-54-21-29. Go north to the grottos 3 km beyond Villars which have wall paintings, tel. 53-54-82-36, one of the most interesting sites in northern Dordogne. Also see the twelfth-century church, the ruins of the twelfth-century Cistercian abbey at Boschaux, and the Renaissance château of Puyguilhem, closed Tuesday, tel. 53-53-44-35. This sixteenth-century chateâu, built in Loire-style, has been well restored. Set in a quiet green valley, it is well worth a visit. For 18 francs you can see the guard room, carved chimneypiece, great hall and carved main staircase.

Continue to Milhac de Nontron, and then east to. **St Jean de Côle**, a really charming little village with Roman hump-backed bridge across the river Côle, twelfth-century château of La Marthonie, open mid-summer, tel. 53-62-30-25, and an eleventh-century priory chapel with a high nave and bell tower. The well-kept village has lovely flowers including, unusually, French bluebells, green lawns, cloisters, and two good restaurants, Auberge du Coq Rouge, tel. 53-62-32-71, and Les Templiers, tel. 53-62-31-75. There is a flower festival between 6th and 8th May. If I were to buy a house in the Dordogne, St Jean de Côle would get my vote! After all it was owned by the English in 1364.

Next go east to **Thiviers** (pop. 4200), a busy market town with truffles, fat poultry, and foie gras available on the Hôtel des Voyageurs' menu, Rue P. Semard, tel. 53-55-09-66. Rather surprisingly Thiviers has a cultural programme including many dances, open air theatre in Place Foch, a 'bourse' for fossils and minerals from 7th-10th July, folklore events in August, rugby matches, fishing competitions and concerts by the 'Joyeux Thiberiens'. Next door to the Syndicat is a small Museum du Foie Gras. The two local châteaux are the twelfth-century Vaucour and La Filolie.

Back to Périgueux via Negrondes on the N21, **Agonac** (pop. 1000) which has an eleventh-century church with buttresses and bell tower, and the river Beauronne valley, to Château L'Evêque and Raymonden.

● **Eastern tour**

The eastern circuit is called 'Au Pays des Pierres' with Hautefort, Badefols and Excideuil châteaux as the main sights. The easy route is on the N89 via St Pierre de Chignac, Fossemagne, Thenon, to Rastignac, along the Vézère valley to Le Lardin St Lazare (Peyraux château) and Terrasson-la-Villedieu, which has two little hotel-restaurants, du Croquant, 2 Rue des Lombards, tel. 53-50-14-09, and Daniel Willer, 6 Avenue Jean-Jaurès, tel. 53-50-06-93. With a population of 6,400, **Terrasson** is a prosperous market town with walnuts, river fish and truffles to offer. The Pont Vieux dates from the twelfth century and the church from the fifteenth century. I am always surprised at the variety of events these Périgordin towns hold. For example, in mid-July is the annual musical festival of Périgord Noir (opera on film in 1989), with fireworks over the Vézère, street balls and other frivolities! The Château de Mellet at Beauregard de Terrasson is worth a visit in midsummer, tel. 53-51-24-94.

Head northwards to Chatres on the minor road D62, then to Badefols d'Ans (pop. 500) owned by the Born family of troubadour fame, with a castle (no visits) now fortunately repaired after the Germans burned it in 1944. Hotel-restaurant Les Tilleuls, tel. 53-51-50-08, is modest and respectable with a 45 franc menu. Now northwest to **Hautefort**, a huge seventeenth-century castle set in a 40 hectare park overlooking the Auvézère valley. It has been repaired after a disastrous fire in 1968, and a guided tour costing 20 francs is recommended, tel. 53-50-51-23. There are ramparts, formal gardens, grey slate roofs and four Loire-style towers. Built originally in the twelfth century, it was involved in the fraternal quarrel between Richard Coeur de Lion and Henry Curtmantel. Altogether it is a château of great dignity and splendour. Among the highlights are the galleries, seventeenth-century chapel, Aubusson tapestries and a small Eugène Le Roy museum. For nearly 15 years whenever we drove by it was enshrouded with scaffolding, but now it is back to its former glory thanks to its owner, Madame La Baronne de Bastard.

Follow the D704 north to Cherveix and **Cubas**, which has two little hotels, Favard, tel. 53-50-41-05, and Les Charmettes, tel. 53-50-56-80. Cubas has a thirteenth-century church, river waterfalls and one of three curious *'Lanternes des Morts'*, cylindrical funeral chapels. We made a little detour west on the D5 to **Tourtoirac** (pop. 750) which has an eleventh-century Benedictine abbey with chapterhouse, ruined cloisters and monks' bread oven. In the cemetery is buried the Dordogne's greatest eccentric and 'unknown' lawyer, who in 1858-60 convinced himself he was another Latin American freedom fighter, and made several determined but foolhardy attempts to conquer (or liberate) Chile, Patagonia and Argentina. He called himself King of Araucania, Orélie-Antoine I. He retired to Tourtoirac and was buried there in 1878. Mad as a hatter but what dreams he must have had. The mercerie in the village is called G. Blondel. Remember Richard Coeur de Lion's troubadour of the same name?

Keep on the D704 to **Lanouaille** (pop. 1000) which makes a good centre for a family holiday. The 40 hectare aqua park at Rouffiac has everything for a young family, tel. 53-52-68-79. Try the *'pain de campagne la Forêt Noire'* in the Patisserie, David Marcel in Lanouaille. The hôtel-restaurant de la Mairie in Angoisse, tel. 53-52-61-04, is good value. To the east in little **Payzac** (pop. 1200) is an eleventh-century bridge, the château, and a large dolmen. From the charcuterie Merillou you can buy *'boudin aux châtaignes'*, a local speciality. The Grand Hôtel des Voyageurs, tel. 53-52-70-10, is

93

good value. The gorges of the river Auvézère between Périgueux and Payac are frequently spectacular.

The alternative to visiting Lanouaille is to head west from the D704 or north from Tourtoirac to **Excideuil** (pop. 1600) on the D705, which has an interesting eleventh-century Château de Talleyrand, built by the Vicomtes de Limoges. It is gradually being repaired and you cannot go inside. However you can enjoy the photogenic view from the riverside. The twelfth-century Benedictine priory is also worth a visit. On 14th July Excideuil has a fête and firework display. On our last visit TV cameras were filming a glamorous wedding party — lunch outside the Chapon Fin and champagne in the château grounds — very romantic! Another château classé is at **St Medard**, 5 km northeast on the D705. This is truffle and *cèpe* country — both on the menu of the Chapon Fin in Excideuil, tel. 53-62-42-38.

Back on the D705, southwest via **Coulaures** with a Romanesque church and châteaux of Conty, sixteenth-century, and La Cousse, eighteenth-century, to Savignac Les Églises and Sarliac-sur-L'Isle, which has a château, Romanesque church and two small hotels, the Chabrol, tel. 53-07-83-39, and Le Nordoc, tel. 53-07-88-61. Next visit the Les Bories fifteenth-century château which is open from 1st July to the end of September, tel. 52-06-00-01. Perched on the river bank it has round towers, a huge keep, a great hall with rich furnishings and tapestries. It is one of the thirty top châteaux in the Dordogne which open their doors for visitors. Back via Antonne-et-Trigonant and Trelissac to Périgueux. The circuit of about 130 km will take about a day.

● **Southwestern tour**

The final circuit is southwest and takes in 35 km of the river l'Isle and valley via Marsac, Razac, Annesse et Beaulieu across the river to **St Astier** (pop. 4900) with twelfth-century church, sixteenth-century clock tower, Puy-Ferrat château, and three small hotels: the Paris, tel. 53-54-10-20; the Domaine de Monciaux, tel. 53-81-97-69; and La Terrasse de Chassaing, tel. 53-54-12-00.

Then go across the river and down the valley via St Léon to Neuvic with two small châteaux, then east on the D39 and

D44 following the little river Vern to Grignols château of the twelfth-fifteenth century, open in summer for visits, tel. 53-54-28-64, then take the D43 across the N21 to Vergt (pop. 1500) noted for its strawberries. There are two little hotels here, La Chaumière, tel. 53-54-90-50, and du Parc, Place Marty, tel. 53-54-78-04

Then north on the D8 to Eglise-Neuve, **Notre Dame de Sanilhac**, which has the Auberge Notre Dame, tel. 53-07-60-69, and finally Atur and Périgueux. The circuit of about 90 km will take half a day.

CHAPTER NINE:
BERGERAC AND LOCAL TOURS

For many years our family regarded **Bergerac** (pop. 30,000) as a large commercial town to be passed through on the way to Bordeaux or Toulouse. But no longer . . . There are three things going for it. It has always been the centre of the wine trade of the Dordogne, the old town has been renovated and there is an exciting programme of annual events.

Bergerac

Once Bergerac was an inland port and the '*ancien port*' still exists two hundred metres west of the main bridge over the river Dordogne. From here my ancestors shipped wine to London in the thirteenth century. The old town covers an area inland from the river about ½ km in width and 1 km across, a quadrilateral in shape. The Rue Neuve d'Argenson on the east flank is the main road from the bridge over the Dordogne into the centre of town towards the *Syndicat d'Initiative* at No 97, tel. 53-57-03-11. They publish an English guide to the old town with its medieval houses, some of wattle and daub, fountains and covered market. In 1622 Cardinal Richelieu ordered the destruction of the ramparts and the filling in of the moats because Bergerac was a Huguenot bastion. St James Church was so named after the thousands of pilgrims who visited it on their way to Compostella. Next door is the Museum of Sacred Art, and a few minutes walk away is the old monastery, the Cloisters des Recollets (now the wine region HQ), and a wine museum, tel. 53-57-80-92. Nearer the river is La Maison Peyrarede, built in 1603, which is now the tobacco museum. Bergerac is the largest producer of tobacco leaf in France, and in the museum you can see pipes, snuffboxes, tobacco graters, Indian peace pipes as well as oil paintings and engravings depicting smoking habits over the years. It is closed on Mondays, tel. 53-57-60-22.

In the Place de la Myrpre is a large white statue to the famous long-nosed Cyrano de Bergerac – the romantic, bibulous town hero. There was a philosopher of that name but no relation who lived in the seventeenth century. The old town is pedestrian only and it takes about two hours to walk around it, longer if you visit the museums en route. Guided visits from 1st July leave from in front of the Church of Notre Dame, usually at 9 a.m. Check with the information office first.

Recently 3½ km of riverside walks have been created along the banks of the Dordogne and regattas take place several times during the summer. The street markets on Wednesdays and Saturdays are a feature and two new ones have started up on the 'rive gauche' in the Place Barbacane and quartier de Naillac. Boat trips on the river to visit the dam downriver take place in the summer, tel. 53-57-02-31. The airclub at the airport of Roumanières offers 'promenades aériennes', tel. 53-57-31-36.

In June there is a Music Festival which takes place over 10 days, early in July a folklore 'spectacle' in the Place St Jacques, and jazz concerts in the Cloisters des Recollets. In August and September there is a curious two-day event, 'Musée de l'humour en Périgord'. The local folklore group is called 'Abeilles bergeracoises' which means busy little bees.

Sporting events include bicycle races, 'concours d'élegance automobile', championship of France at auto-cross, and a rugby challenge cup – all in June. In July there are regattas, firework displays, archery contests, baseball championships, international tennis tournament, night time cycle races, baby shows, dog shows, and the release of 100,000 pigeons back to their native Holland. Much the same happens in August. No wonder annual tourists to Bergerac have tripled in numbers in the last decade.

Modest hotels include Le Moderne (near the railway station), 19 Avenue du 108ème R.I., tel. 53-57-19-62; Le Pozzi (near the Prefecture), 11 Rue du Professeur Pozzi, tel. 53-57-04-68; Le Provence, 2 Place Clairat, tel. 53-57-12-88; Terminus (near the railway station), 17 Avenue du 108ème R.I., tel. 53-57-01-09.

Restaurants worth trying are Le Nautic, 12 Promenade

Pierre Loti, good for river fish; Le Parisien, Rue de la Fonbal-
quine; Le Perroquet, Place Malbec; and Le Poivre et Sel. Les
St Jacques near the church has a 58 franc menu — next to
'Hankeys of Bergerac Tea Rooms'!

Bergerac is a sensible base if you want to tour the west and
southwest of the Dordogne. For the young there are discotheques, two large swimming pools, a riding club, parachuting
school, cycling and canoeing activities. There are several
regional tours which I have tried out. Local bus tours from the
SNCF and Tourist Office are organised in July and August to
the Forêt de Bessede (Château de Lanquais, St Avit-Senieur
and Cadouin, 70 francs), to the Gouffre de Proumeyssac
(Lalinde, Le Bugue, Cingle de Limeuil and Tremolat, 75
francs), and Châteaux and Bastides (Beaumont, Monpazier
and Biron, 70 francs), tel. 53-58-28-74.

● Prehistoric tour

The prehistoric route starts east on the D660 through Creysse,
Monleydier to Lalinde, Mauzac, Tremolat, Limeuil and Le
Bugue. The main sites are covered in Chapter Thirteen. After
Thonac and Losse turn west on minor roads to Fleurac and
the grotto of Rouffignac, and on the D45 to Vergt, a *bastide*
town. The D21 via the chateau of La Gaubette and Mon-
trastruc links up with the N21 and brings you back into
Bergerac. Allow a full day if it is your first visit to the
prehistoric sites between Les Eyzies and Montignac.

● Bastide towns tour

There are twenty *bastide* towns and villages in the Dordogne,
half of them sponsored by the Count of Toulouse, Alphonse
de Poitiers, in the middle and late thirteenth century. As the
French king Saint Louis' brother, his responsibility was to keep
the English at bay. These rectangular fortified towns built on
a grid basis with central square, fortified church and arcades,
were designed with their narrow streets for defensive reasons.
For commercial purposes they were built near a main road or
river or preferably both. As soon as a French *bastide* was built
the English responded by building one of their own. But if you
look at a map the English *bastides* (Villefranche-de-Lonchat,
La Bastide, Puyguilhem, Fonroque, Lalinde, Molières, Beau-

mont, Roquepine and Monpazier) were in the middle of a sandwich. Three French *bastides* were on the north side (Vergt, Domme, Ste Foy-la-Grande), and on the south side Eymet, Castillionnès, Villeréal and Villefranche-du-Périgord. Very odd!

A historian or architect on holiday making a *'circuit des bastides'* should go west to **Ste Foy-la-Grande** (pop. 3000), a *bastide* town founded in 1255 by Alphonse de Poitiers. The Place de la Mairie with its old houses and covered arcades conjures up memories of the past. Although in the department of the Gironde, you will eat and drink well at the Boule d'Or, tel. 53-46-00-76, and Vieille Auberge, tel. 53-46-04-78. Bisected by the river Dordogne there are delightful views and walks. The rectangular grid of streets is on the south side.

Villefranche-de-Lonchat, 40 km northwest on the D9, was built by our King Edward III as a *bastide* town. It has an excellent wine co-op and two châteaux nearby, Montaigne's 12 km south, and 5 km east that of Gurson, near a large lake. **La Bastide** lies 15 km southeast of Sainte Foy-la-Grande, a small hamlet which was also an English *bastide* although there is little left now to show for it. Seven km due south is Puyguilhem, and then Fonroque, two more little villages, erstwhile English *bastides*. Castles and wine co-ops abound here so there is a lot to look at − the châteaux of Theobon, Bridoire and Monbazillac and the vineyard villages of Saussignac, Sigoulès and Monbazillac again.

Eymet (pop. 3000) was a French-owned *bastide* 5 km southeast of Fonroque on the D933. Being on the main road from Bergerac to Marmande it prospered, whereas with the benefit of hindsight the three English *bastides* were badly sited. Eymet is also on the river Dropt so there were two sources of revenue. The Place Central is arcaded and has several medieval houses. The castle-keep (*donjon*) dates from the fourteenth century. It is well worth a visit. One eats well at both the Hôtel Beauséjour, tel. 53-23-81-25, and du Château, tel. 53-23-81-35, particularly on Thursday, market day, when truffles, *cèpes, foie gras* and plums may be on the menu. There are pretty gardens opposite the town hall, the gently flowing river, palm trees, a small prehistory museum, tel. 53-23-80-16 − yes, Eymet must be visited.

To the east is **Castillonès** (pop. 2000) in the department of the Lot-et-Garonne, a French bastide town. It is on a crossroads of the N21 with the D1 and D2 and has prospered. It has the Hôtel de Europe, tel. 53-36-86-31. Roquépine 15 km northeast is a small English bastide, and Villereal, southeast on the D207, was a French bastide (back in the Lot-et-Garonne), and has the Hôtel de l'Europe, 1 Rue Mirabeau, tel. 53-36-00-35.

Monpazier (pop. 550) is 15 km east northeast on the D104, a centre of four roads and on the river Dropt, so although small it has survived happily. King Edward I founded it on 7th January 1284 but it changed hands several times in the Hundred Years War. One of the three best preserved *bastides* in the Dordogne, it still has three fortified gateways, a rectangular street grid with several medieval houses, the arcaded Place Centrale, a thirteenth century chapterhouse, sixteenth century fortified church of St Dominique, and a covered market with old measures. A fair is held on the third Thursday of each month. Try the Hôtel de France, tel. 53-22-60-06, and the Restaurant de la Bastide, the former at No 21 and the latter No 52, Rue St Jacques.

The real glutton for punishment will visit the eastern sector *bastides*: Montcabrier, Villefranche du Périgord, Domme, Bretenoux, Rudelle and Labastide-Murat, but in truth these are best visited from Sarlat (see next chapter).

Go from Monpazier northwest on the D660 to **Beaumont-du-Périgord**, another 1272 English bastide town (pop. 1300). Most of the ramparts have been destroyed but many arcaded houses remain, as does St Front church built in the same year by the English which is well fortified with four corner defensive towers. The local information office in Rue Romieu is very proud of **their** *'bastide anglaise'* founded by Lucas de Thaney, Seneschal of Guyenne *'au nom du roi d'Angleterre Edouard Ier'*. The street plan shows the original rectangular grid with the Place Centrale and Place Vieille, also the thirteenth century fortified Porte de Lazier. It is a busy market town near a river, and one eats well at the Hôtel des Voyageurs, also known as Chez Popaul, tel. 53-22-31-11 (very good hors d'oeuvres from Jean-Paul Delbos), and at Hôtel-Restaurant des Arcades, tel. 53-22-30-31.

The way to **Molières** (pop. 300) is via St Avit-Senieur with its huge fortified church, partly eleventh century, mainly fourteenth century, and Cadouin's great abbey is temptingly close. Although Molières is an unfinished English bastide with a fortified Gothic church, it is not worth a detour by itself, but add St Avit and Cadouin and there is no real choice!

From Molières go west via Bourniquel to the delightful fifteenth century château of Bannes, which was built by the bishop of Sarlat. Perched on a hill it is uncertain whether it existed for military, ecclesiastical or social reasons. A pity it is not open to the public but with its many circular towers, pepperpot roofs, moat and drawbridge it is worth visiting just to see the outside. Just 2 km north is the sixteenth century Châteaux de Bayac with machiolated towers.

The final *bastide* town on this circuit is **Lalinde** (pop. 3000) with two major châteaux nearby: Lanquais, fourteenth century, southwest, closed Tuesday, tel. 53-25-02-04; and Baneuil, fourteenth century, northwest, open August, tel. 53 -61-08-31. The *bastide* was founded by our King Edward III, but little remains except the rectangular pattern of the streets, some ramparts and the western Porte Romane. See also the twelfth century chapel of St Front and the château of Laffinoux. The week of frivolity is the first in July with *'fête votive'*, a marathon race and fishing competition. Perhaps the Hotel du Périgord, Place du 14 Juillet, tel. 53-61-19-86 will have still *'truite meunière'* on their menu? And so back to Bergerac.

● Wine tour

The circuit *'des vignobles'* is covered in Chapter Twelve with visits to Monbazillac, Côtes de Bergerac, Pécharmont, Montravel and Côtes de Saussignac, including the wine co-operatives in Bergerac, Monbazillac, Sigoulès etc.

● Gallo-Roman tour

The circuit 'Gallo-Roman' is to the west along the D32 to **Le Fleix**, a lovely little village, a Gallo-Roman site where arrowheads and tools have been discovered from the second to the fourth centuries. There are still many medieval houses here and several artisans in the Rue des Canons. Then west to **Montcaret** on the D936 past Velines, where there is a Gallo-

Roman villa with mosaics and thermal bath with fish designs. Probably part of a Roman aqueduct here too. Open 1st April to the end of September, tel. 53-08-00-94. You do not need an excuse to head north to Montaigne country to see the land of that great Périgord philosopher, Michel de Montaigne. And there are several wine co-ops who will be pleased to see you!

CHAPTER TEN:
SARLAT AND LOCAL TOURS

My favourite town in the Dordogne region is Sarlat with its charming medieval old quarters, cathedral and curiosities. It has a population of 10,000 and is crammed full of tourists in the summer months. The town makes an excellent base from which to visit prehistoric sites on the Vézère, *bastides* (Domme, Villefranche du Périgord, Monpazier), and the castles along the banks of the Dordogne. Its only snag is that the main traffic goes down the Rue de la République (known as *La Traverse*) straight through the centre of town, as there is no effective bypass. It also hosts a lively programme of events and activities.

Sarlat

Charlemagne in the eighth century sponsored a Benedictine monastery which became part of the Cluny order in the tenth century. St Bernard, according to legend, returning from Crusade in 1147, accomplished a miracle by providing loaves of bread for the needy. The English army occupied Sarlat for a decade (1360-70) before Du Guesclin re-conquered the town. My wretched Huguenot forebears did a lot of senseless damage in the wars of religion and scattered the bones and ashes of the fifth-century Saint Sacerdos in the river Dordogne. Sarlat slumbered and decayed for centuries as the river boat traffic seized up and the railway came and went! The city fathers got their act together in 1962 under the Loi Malraux and, helped by the state, repaired and restored the old town to its present beauty.

First of all find the tourist office in the centre of the old town on the east side of *La Traverse*. It occupies one of the most attractive medieval houses, the Hôtel de Maleville in the Place de la Liberté, tel. 53-59-27-67. The staff are very helpful and provide a street plan which is indispensable, since every corner and narrow street has something of interest to see. A walking tour of 20 items will take about three hours, and guided tours in summer start at the tourist office. The cathedral of St Sacerdos, built in 1504, is a good place to begin. The bishopric founded in 1317 was of course abolished during the French Revolution. Adjoining it is the old bishops, palace, now the theatre, and opposite is the beautiful house, built in 1525 by Antoine de la Boetie, where Montaigne's friend Étienne was born five years later. Built in Italian Renaissance style with mullioned windows and steep gabled roof, it is indeed photogenic.

At the back of the cathedral in a small garden is the mysterious Lanterne des Morts, built about 1175. The cylindrical stone tower has a steep conical top and two floors with occasional slit windows, and is probably a funeral chapel. Possibly St Bernard's miraculous bread loaves were conceived here. The main sixteenth-century houses to look at are the 'Hôtels' des Oies (in Goose Square for the Saturday markets), Selve de Plamon (partly fourteenth-century and used by the cloth workers, guild), de Grezel with typical *lauze* (heavy rectangular slates) roof, de Betou Magnanat, Omeja, d'Autrery, de Vassal, and other buildings in the Rue des Consuls and Rue des Armes. Tucked away are several fountains (Sainte Marie in a grotto), shrines, old gateways, and several parks including the Jardin Publique (ideal for picnics). On my last visit I found a large manor house/small seventeenth-century château with rose gardens for sale in the Rue de la Salamandre near the Presidial where King Henri II dispensed justice.

On the west side of *La Traverse* are to be found Ste Clair's Convent and cloisters, the Chapelle des Penitents Blancs, two watch towers (Guet and Bourreau) and several hundred metres of ramparts. The church of Sainte-Marie and the Chapelle des Pénitents Bleus (an unusual order) should also be visited. There are two museums in Sarlat, that of Sacred Art in the Chapel of the White Penitents and, rather incongruously, the Musée-Aquarium, tel. 53-59-44-58 in the northwest of town, open June-September, which originated in a study of the Dordogne river (life of the fish, the fishermen and their boats). Thirty freshwater fish can be seen, some migratory (salmon, sturgeon, lampreys), some sedentary (perch, pike, bleak).

Modest hotels include the Beauséjour, Route de Souillac, tel. 53-59-37-00; Lion d'Or, 48 Avenue Gambetta, tel. 53-59-00-83; and Marcel, 8 Avenue Selves, tel. 53-59-21-98. Most of the restaurants in the old town ought to charge extra for the sheer beauty of their ambience. The Café la Boetie offers Périgourdin soup in its 50 franc menu; Le Moulin du Roi is tucked away near the tourist office in a quiet golden corner and offers 'cassoulet périgourdin' in their 65 franc menu. The Restaurant Gueule et Gosier, quiet and near the Mairie, had 'pâté au foie gras' and 'manchon de canard' in their 60 franc menu when I was there.

Sarlat is full of gastronomic shops offering delectables – foie gras and confits in jars and tins, walnut oil, truffles, wines of the regions. A ceramic artist has a permanent exhibition in her atelier – Patricia Berkenza, Rue Escande. Various dance and musical events or summer courses are held, mainly in July. The main folklore group, Peiraguda and Les Pastoureaux Sarladais, perform during the summer, as do Les Quadrilles Sarladais and Les Baladins du Dimanche. Each summer in July and August, there is a Festival des Jeux du Théâtre, and 'Musique en Sarladais'. Also 'Son et Lumière' in August, as well as marathons, night cycle races, and something of everything on 14th July (fireworks, a ball, horse races). Always something for the family to watch.

Bicycles can be hired from L'Aventure à Vélo on the route de Bergerac, tel. 53-31-24-18, and 'Hep-Excursions' offer tours of Périgord in minibuses, specifically on the 'petits chemins', tel. 53-28-10-04. The Monday tour of Quercy including Rocamadour and Padirac costs 130 francs; Tuesday either to Lascaux or the Valley of the Dordogne 95 francs each; Wednesday is artisan day. For 125 francs you can visit a glass-blower, a goose farm (you may not appreciate the animals being force-fed) artisan confiseur (nuts and chocolate), a walnut oil mill, Grottos of Cougnac, and Château of La Roussie. A very interesting mixture. Thursday is a prehistory tour to Les Eyzies, Prehistoric Park, St Léon de Vézère (that pretty little village), Castelmerle prehistoric village, Château of Commarque and the village de Bories (dry stone bee-shaped shepherds' houses). Price 125 francs. Friday is château day, and the Saturday tour goes to Cadouin plus three châteaux. The tours are run by M. et Madame Gérard Dunoyer. It is an inexpensive and interesting way of seeing the region.

Other local artisans and producers you can visit in or near Sarlat include two distilleries — Salamandre at Temniac (3 km north, tel. 53-59-10-00) and Mazelaygue at Madrazès (2 km south, tel. 53-59-31-10) — M. Tache's Moulin à Huile de Noix at Sainte-Nathalène (8.5 km east, tel. 53-59-22-08), and three artisans conserviers, M. Gerardin at Vitrac, M. Crouzel at Le Temple and M. Lembert at Beynac.

The local tourist office print a useful free leaflet 'Circuits Touristiques' complete with maps. It is very detailed (in French).

There are four tours.

(i) The first tour to the Dordogne valley takes in Domme, Castelnaud (open all year), Les Milandes (open all year) and Beynac castle (open all year). Although only 30 km it could take a day as there is a lot to see. You could extend the trip further south to encompass Belvès, a little hill-top town with seven towers and the Hôtel de France, tel. 53-29-11-80.

(ii) The western prehistory circuit of 50 km includes Marquay (thirteenth-century fortified church), the château of Laussel, thirteenth-century Château de Commarque, Abri du Cap Blanc, Les Eyzies, Grotto de Font de Gaume (closed Tuesdays), and back by the château of Beyssac, Le Gîte à Fossiles (Paleolithic centre), Château du Roc and Château de Puymartin (open April–September).

(iii) The third circuit of 60 km to the valley of the Vézère is initially north to St Geniès (château, Romanesque church), to St Amand de Coly (twelfth century fortified abbey), west to Montignac to see Lascaux II (closed Mondays out of season), the gisement of Regourdou, as well as the Museum Eugène Le Roy in Montignac. Head south on the D65 parallel to the river Vézère to the Château de Losse (open July-September), to Thonac and the Centre d'Art Prehistorique du Thot (closed Monday out of season). On to Sergeac, museum of

Castlemerle (closed Wednesdays), St Léon sur Vézère, the troglodyte fortress village of La Roque Saint Christophe, the *gisements* of Moustier and the troglodyte village of La Madeleine (closed Tuesdays) and back via the D47 to Sarlat.

(iv) The eastern circuit to Quercy, Rocamadour and Padirac is rather longer — 150 km. First by the D704 and D703 go to Souillac — the château of Rouffillac amongst the green chestnut trees — Peyrillac — Cazoules (now in the Lot department), and a visit to the Abbey of Sainte Marie in Souillac. Briefly stay on the N20 before turning off along the river road east — Pinsac — the splendid château of La Treyne and that of Le Belcastle (outside only) to the fourteenth-century fortified mill of Cougnaguet — over the bridge of the Ouysse to Lacave. There you go by electric train and lift to see the grottos. Next the D247 to Rocamadour where it is best to leave your car at the top of the hill at l'Hospitalet. A visit to the cluster of noble churches, chapels and shrines, plus the castle at the summit will take you a good half a day but is well worth it. Then go on to Padirac to see the famous '*gouffre*' and underground river, on the D673 then the D38 to the villages of Alvignac and Autoire (with its Château des Anglais), the castle and grotto at Montal, the town of St Céré in the valley of the Bave, northwest to Castelnau and the river road west to Carennac (church, cloister and Fénelon's home), to Floirac, N140 to Martel and D703 to Souillac and back to Sarlat. I have condensed this tour because in the next chapter it is covered in more detail.

To sum up, the circuit-tours available from Sarlat are in my view the most interesting in the whole of the Dordogne. You can visit the castles on the Dordogne, prehistoric remains with 19 troglodyte forts on the Vézère, bastides in the southwest (Domme, Villefranche du Périgord, Montcabrier, Monpazier and Labastide-Murat). In fact, the only missing ingredient is a wine tour which is best done from Bergerac.

CHAPTER ELEVEN:
EASTERN DORDOGNE VALLEY

The continuation of the river valley into the northern sector of the neighbouring department of the Lot, known to the French as Quercy, contains a plethora of outstandingly pretty villages, châteaux, several abbeys and churches, grottos, countryside for walking (GR 6 and 64), riding and canoe-kayak activities. And of course you can eat and drink as well here as in the main Dordogne department!

There are three towns where one can base a stay of a few days, as well as a dozen villages. The towns are **Gourdon** in the west (pop. 5000), **Souillac** near the Dordogne and Corrèze rivers (pop. 4000), and **St Céré** to the east on the river Bave (pop. 4200). I would recommend that you avoid Rocamadour, which has fifteen hotels, unless it is out of season, since the religious complex of seven chapels/churches becomes overcrowded very easily. In high season Souillac too, with its eighteen hotels, is just as bad as the traffic on the N20 passes straight through the centre and many tourists stop off en route. In season I would suggest either Gourdon or St Céré which are less obviously tourist-orientated, and amongst the many small villages either Carennac, Lacave, St Sozy or Gintrac on the river, or you can get very good value inland, at Alvignac or Miers.

For caravan-campers I have listed campsites by area and by classification — roughly half by rivers, and half in the hinterland (see Chapter Four). In addition there are holiday villages with chalets etc at Gluges (near Martel), tel. 65-37-33-70 and Gourdon, tel. 65-41-05-15.

The main sights in Haut-Quercy are shown below — roughly in order of importance, This is very subjective, I know, but I believe it may be of help.

1. The pilgrimage site of Rocamadour – the ultimate religious and historical village clinging to a steep cliff with 216 penitential steps, black Virgin, Durandel sword, treasury, crypt, basilica, ninth-century clock, frescoes, son-et-lumière, and a castle at the top of the hill, tel. 65-33-60-73 for more information.

2. The chasm (almost a black hole) of Padirac, over 100 metres deep with kilometres of underground river and lakes, tel. 65-33-64-56.

3. The grottos of Lacave, 12 underground caves with thousands of stalactites, and subterranean lakes entered by electric train plus a lift to take you up inside to explore, tel. 65-37-87-03. (There are three other local grottos — des Merveilles near Rocamadour, tel. 65-33-67-92; Presque near St Céré, tel. 65-38-07-44; and Cougnac near Gourdon, tel. 65-41-06-11.)

4. The châteaux roughly in order of importance are the huge red stone eleventh-century Castelnau-Bretenoux (closed Tuesdays), tel. 65-38-52-04; La Treyne near Lacave, tel. 65-32-66-66; Montal, sixteenth-century near St Céré, tel. 65-38-13-72; and Rocamadour, tel. 65-33-63-29, all open to the public April – October.

5. The village of Carennac beside the river Dordogne, one of 'les plus beaux villages de France', with Fénelon's old priory, Romanesque cloisters and turreted manor houses. Look for the Tympanum of St Pierre in the priory-church. Try trout stuffed with crayfish in the hotel-restaurant Fénelon if it is still on the menu.

6. The fortified fourteenth-Century village of Loubressac, just east of Padirac, with panoramic views over the river valleys of the Bave and Dordogne. Nearby Autoire is even more beautiful.

7. The twelfth-century Roman-Byzantine abbey church of St Martin in Souillac with the Roman sculptures of the prophet Isaiah and 'Le Trumeau' on the inside doorway.

8. The pretty medieval town of Gourdon built on a hill.

9. The historical small town (pop. 1400) of Martel with its seven towers, 15 km north east from Souillac.

10. Rocamadour has two museums — of Sacred Art, tel. 65-33-63-29, and Waxworks of Roland le Preux. It also has a few curiosities. Near Rocamadour is a monkey reserve known as La Forêt des Singes. In 10 hectares of woods and parkland 150 Barbary apes ('*macaques*') have a protected colony, tel. 65-33-62-72. The entry is on the CD36. Nearby is the Butterfly Park (*Le Jardin des Papillons*). Price 20 francs. Here you can see varieties of butterflies from all over the world fluttering amid exotic plants and flowers around a waterfall and rivulets. The fourteenth-century fortified mill Cougnaguet, near Calès, is worth a visit.

St Céré is said to have small vineyards producing '*vin paille*', which I failed to track down. Perhaps a reader will identify the villages producing it? At Miers-les-Eaux and Alvignac-les-Eaux, erstwhile spa villages, there is still a locally bottled mineral water conferring untold benefits!

Gourdon

The old town on top of the hill has many medieval houses, the 1304 twin-towered church of St Pierre, a fortified thirteenth-century town gate (Porte Cavaignac), arcades, and narrow streets with emotive names — La Bastidette, Rue Zig-Zag, Rue de l'Iffernet (prison), Chapel du Majou, Maison du Sénechal, Rue Tortue, Rue de Roc, Rue des Consuls — to mention some of them. The views from the ramparts at the top are superb. Unfortunately Louis XIII had the seigneurial castle of Lauzières-Themines destroyed in 1619.

In the seventeenth century Gourdon was the centre of a school of baroque sculpture famous in the region. The master wood-engraver was Jean Tournie (1652-1702), who produced pulpits, mantelpieces in the Maison des Consuls and the reredos wooden statues in the churches of Notre Dame, des Cordeliers, Nôtre Dame des Neiges and St Pierre. Each summer for two weeks there is an international music festival in the Gourdon churches.

Gourdon is a sub-prefecture town on a crossroads with the

D704 25 km southeast from Sarlat and the D673 running west-east to Payrac and Rocamadour. It is also on the main railway line from Paris — Souillac and south to Cahors. The rivers of le Bléou, le Céou, la Melve and la Marcillande provide freshwater fish and campsites. The grotto of Cougnac is 2 km north near the D704.

There are several modest hotels including Le Nouvel, 1 Bd Madeleine, tel. 65-41-00-23, and Le Terminus, 7 Ave de la Gare, tel. 65-41-03-29. The restaurant Le Croque Note in Rue Jean Jaurès, tel. 65-41-25-29 has *'laperau confit à la gràtne de moutarde'* on its 74 franc menu. Both hotels have *prix fixe* meals of around 60 francs. The tourist office is in an old house on the Allées de la République, tel. 65-41-06-40. The cycle club will rent you a *'vélo'*, and the horse-riding club a suitable nag. Fish in the nearby lake of Laumel.

St Céré

Due east of Gourdon via Le Vigan, Payrac, Rocamadour, Alvignac, Padirac and Montal — some 62 km — is St Céré, situated on the D673 and D914 and the rail line Brive-Aurillac. The river La Bave runs through the town which has many medieval houses (Miramon, Ambert), the twelfth-century church of Ste-Spérie and Church of Récollets. The old streets are Rue Paramette, Rue du Mazel, Rue St-Cyr, Bd. Carnot and Place du Mercadial. The Saturday markets and the larger fairs held on the first and third Wednesday of each month are worth attending. The town took its name from the Christian martyr Sainte Spérie, who was killed in AD 780 and the fortress of Saint-Serenus, which dates from the sixth century, and is now the Château de Saint-Laurent. The grand remains, with two huge towers, overlook the town, 3 km to the north. Five bridges cross the river Bave and link the old town with the new. There is a pleasant walk along the Quai des Récollets. There are statues to the many prominent citizens; Marshal Canrobert, Bourseul (an inventor of the telephone), François Maynard (a poet) and Jean Lurcat (of tapestry and cartoon fame). His collection of tapestries can be seen in the Galerie du Casino. The Maison Louis XIII, now a bank, is one of the most elegant buildings. In mid-summer (14th July — 15th August) there

111

is the musical festival of St Céré, tel. 65-38-29-08. The tourist office is in the Place de la République, tel. 65-38-11-85. There is also a vintage car museum, tel. 65-38-15-72.

There are four little hotels: La Truite Dorée, Ave. Charles Bourseul, tel. 65-38-17-54; du Parc, Rue Faubourg Lascabannes, tel. 65-38-17-29; du Quercy, Ave. Charles Bourseul, tel. 65-38-04-83 and Chez Pierrette, Ave. Dr Roux, tel. 65-38-14-77. They all have restaurants which serve river trout. The Au Coin de Pêche, 11 Bd. Gambetta, tel. 65-38-22-89 will supply all you need for a fishing holiday and teach you how to fly-fish!

It is also good walking country. The tourist office can give you information and arrange for your basic luggage/tent to be transported ahead of you (possibly by a friendly ass!) The castles of St Laurent and Montal are within easy walking distance and the grotto of Presque-St Medard is only 6 km away. Autoire and Loubressac are the two prettiest local villages both within a 10 km distance due west.

Souillac

This is another town which, although noticeably glossy and prosperous, makes me feel guilty every time I go there. Twice in the Hundred Years War it was taken and sacked by the English troops and again by the Huguenots protesting at the end of the sixteenth century. It is amazing how the main sight, its great abbey, still stands so proudly thanks to repairs in 1835-8. Set 1½ km north of the river Dordogne, Souillac is unfortunately bisected by the N20. Fortunate for its citizens because it brings prosperity in the shape of thousands of tourists to its 18 hotels and pleasant campsites on both banks of the river. There is something for everyone here. For the active there is tennis, golf, riding, swimming, cycling, walks and canoe-kayak, while more sedentary motorists can visit a score of castles and grottos within easy reach. The standard of cuisine is high — liver pie with truffles, goose confit, *cabécou* du Causse (cheese), *pastis* (pastry with either meat or fruit) and many other local dishes to delight the palate.

The tourist office is in the main street near the Abbey, Bd. L-J Malvy, tel. 65-37-81-56. Town walking tours start there. The National Museum of Automates is also in the Place de l'Abbaye, tel. 65-37-07-07. Quercy-Land is a sporting park for the young with minigolf, moto-cross, karting, trampoline, bicycle riding, *jeux nautiques* etc, tel. 65-32-72-61. In mid-summer the town hosts a jazz festival.

There are several small hotel-restaurants; Le Beffroi, 6 Place St. Martin, tel. 65-37-80-33; Le Redouille, 28 Avenue de Toulouse, tel. 65-37-87-25; and, without restaurants La Cascade, Rue de Timbergues, tel. 65-37-84-49 and L'Escale, 4 Avenue Général de Gaulle, tel. 65-37-03-96.

For serious walkers there are well-marked tracks, known as Grandes Randonnées, which criss-cross the area. The GR6 works its way eastwards from Les Eyzies to Sarlat and Souillac, Pinsac, Lacave, Rocamadour, Gramat and southeast to Figeac. From Sarlat the GR64 goes southeast to Groléjac, Gourdon, Le Vigan, Reilhaguet to Rocamadour. The GR46 comes in from the north, Brive – Turenne – Sarrazac to Martel and Gluges and south to Rocamadour. The GR652 comes in from the northeast at Laval-de-Céré, Cornac – north of Saint Céré – to Loubressac – Carennac and west to Montvalent. The appropriate Topo-Guides are GR36/636 Ref. 359; GR6/64 Ref. 605 and GR652 Ref. 614.

For animal lovers Padirac has a zoo, tel. 65-33-64-91; Rocamadour, in addition to butterflies and monkeys, has an eagle sanctuary 'Rocher des Aigles', tel. 65-33-65-45. Horse riding stables are to be found at Pinsac (Ferme du Boumet, tel. 65-32-23-94), Lacave (Les Attelages de Bellemire, tel. 65-37-05-85), Souillac (Club Hippique Souillagais, tel. 65-32-64-62 and Centre Equestre du Gachou, tel. 65-32-27-17) and Vayrac (Château de Blanat, tel. 65-32-49-17).

Bicycle hire from the following places: Gourdon (Bigot, Avenue Cavaignac, tel. 65-41-11-83 and SNCF 65-41-02-19), Rocamadour (SNCF 65-33-63-05), Souillac (SNCF 65-32-78-21 and Bicausse, Place de la Halle 65-37-03-64), Saint Céré (M. Saint Chamand, Rue Faidherbe, tel. 65-38-03-23). Canoe-kayaks can be hired at Gluges (Copeyre, tel. 65-37-33-51), Creysse (tel.

113

65-32-20-40), Lacave (UCPA tel. 65-37-01-45) and Gluges-Martel (Activité-Canoe, tel. 65-37-33-70).

Swimming pools to be found at Bretenoux-Biars; Gourdon; Gramat; Payrat; Souillac; Saint Céré and Vayrac. River bathing 'beaches' at Creysse, Floirac, Gintrac, Gluges, Martel, Pinsac, Puybrun, Souillac, St Denis and Vayrac — all on the river Dordogne. Artificial lakes and lake bathing at Alvignac, Gourdon (two) and Le Vigan.

Discotheques for the young at Gourdon (Le Semaphore), Puybrun (La Guinguette), Martel (Auberge de Copeyre), Miers (La Source Salmière), Padirac (Le Troglo, of course), Rocamadour (La Hulotte), Saint Céré (Le Casino), Vayrac (L'Oppidum) and Le Vigan (Le Rétro-Negrefeuille).

Part Three:
Specialist Tours

CHAPTER TWELVE:
WINE TOURS

Just to the east of the famous Bordeaux wine growing area, a cluster of 93 villages around Bergerac produce nearly 50 million bottles of wine each year. The climate is mild and the vines are spread out on terraces on both sides of the river Dordogne. The British and Belgian markets each import three million bottles a year and tie for second place well behind the Netherlands, which takes nearly double. Nearly every UK high street supermarket and wine store stock Bergerac and Monbazillac wines.

Nearly two thousand years ago the poet Ausonius was declaiming the excellence of the vines which bordered the river Dordogne, probably introduced by the Romans when they first arrived in the area around 60 BC. Ruthless invaders – such as the Franks, Visigoths, Arabs and Normans – sailed their small ships up the rivers Gironde and Dordogne and pillaged the countryside in their summer campaigning, but probably were gone by vintage time! As usual the monks (*les moines*) in the local abbeys encouraged wine growing for their sacramental wine (and for themselves) and the local *seigneurs* followed suit. The Prior of Pomport and his immediate neighbour, the Seigneur de Montcuq, were the main early vineyard owners who sold their surplus production to the bourgeois of Bergerac (10 km to the north).

For three centuries from 1150-1453 AD the wine growing area belonged to the English crown. When Prince of Wales, the future King Henry III, authorised the wine growing and selling franchise of Bergerac wines there was soon a healthy export trade to London. My ancestors trading in London were wine merchants of La Réole who, in the thirteenth century, purchased wines from the Gironde and the Dordogne, shipped them in cask from Bordeaux, and sold the wines profitably on arrival. All that changed when the French ended the Hundred Years War in 1453 at Castillon. Trade with England diminished and the Dutch imported wines from the southwest of France to be distilled into 'genever' gin.

Up to the Middle Ages the wines of Bergerac were mainly to be found on the north side of the river. However, a new government tax persuaded the monks to plant on the south (untaxed) side of the river! There they discovered by mistake a humid climate which encouraged the wine bunches to rot — the Noble Rot or *Botrytis cinerea*. As the grapes lost their water content, the sugar that remained was high and the great sweet white wine of Monbazillac was developed. From the eleventh century the monks exploited bit by bit this unusual wine. When the Huguenot inhabitants of Bergerac were forced to emigrate for religious reasons to the Netherlands in the sixteenth and seventeenth centuries, they decided they needed their own familiar wines. That is the reason why the twentieth-century exports of Bergerac and Monbazillac wines to that country are so high.

Francis I, King of France in 1520, authorised the wines of Bergerac to be shipped throughout the year on the river Dordogne and eventually exports to the English market picked up again. The *Consuls* (councillors) of Bergerac insisted on strict quality control, and the local history books attest that in 1352, 1376, 1520, 1558 and 1668 the Bergerac wines were rigorously checked by the judicial authorities.

Despite religious wars and the French Revolution the vineyards continued to prosper, until in 1870 the dreaded phylloxera disease struck across Europe. For 20 years wine production suffered terribly. All the vineyards were replanted with the new tough resistant American stock, and in 1936 Bergerac wines were awarded A.O.C. standards.

More recently, in 1953, the Conseil Interprofessionnel des Vins de la Région de Bergerac was created, and it is now at the Maison du Vin, 2 Place du Dr Cayla, 24100 Bergerac, tel. 53-57-12-57. They have four main responsibilities. These are careful quality control through their oenological laboratory, advice to growers, a certain amount of pricing guidance and publicity. The council consists of eight growers, two members of the influential Cave Co-operatives, four wine wholesaler members, one hotelier and one wine agent, plus the president of the Institut National des Appellations d'Origine (I.N.A.O.)

Types of wine

It is quite a complicated area in that there are four different A.O.C. (Appellation Contrôlé) wines and many growers own various separate vineyards which make one or more A.O.C. wines. The big co-ops make all four varieties.

Bergerac which includes Bergerac rouge, Côtes de Bergerac, Bergerace rosé, Bergerac blanc sec and Côtes Bergerac Moëlleux (sweet white wine from Saussignac). Production: rouge 200,000 hls; Côtes de Bergerac 25,000 hls; rosé 3000 hls; blanc sec 50-70,000 hls; Saussignac 2500 hls.

Monbazillac blanc. Production 50-60,000 hls a year.

Montravel Montravel blanc, Côtes Montravel, Haut Montravel blanc. Production 30-35,000 hls a year.

Pécharmant rouge. Production 8-10,000 hls a year.
Note: 1 hls = about 11 dozen bottles of wine.

The total of about 350-400,000 hectolitres is now split equally between red/rosé and white, and just under a third is exported outside France. Nearly half of the total production is controlled by large co-ops who have been very beneficial to the region. Many 'vignerons' own small vineyards with under five hectares (12½ acres) – and they do not have any marketing facilities, unless the family own their own restaurants! The co-op buys either the grapes or the wine at vintage time, then blends, matures and bottles. Their quality control is excellent and this combined with bottling and labelling techniques produces a very drinkable bottle of wine at a reasonable price. The wine vignerons share in the profits pro rata according to their individual production.

The largest co-ops are at Monbazillac, with 150 *vigneron* members, and Unidor, which has 8 smaller co-ops grouped

117

together. Both make and sell about five million bottles a year. All the co-ops together account for 40% of the production of Bergerac wines.

Planning your tours

For *'amateurs des vins'* the best plan is to base oneself in Bergerac for a few days, perhaps at the Hôtel Le Pécharmant or Hôtel Parisien, and then divide the wine tours into four segments, north west, north east, south west and south east. The co-ops do not need advance warning of your visit, but it is always advisable to telephone the châteaux owners to make an appointment. Be prepared to buy a case of six or twelve bottles.

● North western tour

The D936 on the south side of the river Dordogne takes one westwards to the Montravel A.O.C. area. At Sainte Foy-la-Grande the road crosses the river and immediately on the north side is the Montravel region, a rectangle of 20 km by 10. The main villages are Vélines (pop. 1000), Montcaret (pop. 100) which has a wine co-op and liqueur distillery, St Michel de Montaigne (pop. 300), Bonneville (pop. 200) with another co-op, Montpeyroux (pop. 400), Saint-Vivien (pop. 250), Fouqueyrolles (pop. 400) and Saint Méard-de-Gurçon (pop. 800).

In 1307 the 19 parishes of Montravel were owned by the Archbishop of Bordeaux, Arnaud de Canteloup. All the wines of Montravel are white. Montravel blanc is dry and the Ugni grape gives it a certain acidity. Haut-Montravel and Côtes de Montravel are both sweet white wines. They are all a blend of grape varieties called Sémillon, Muscadelle and Sauvignon. The dry wines are best drunk young, whereas the sweet will age in bottle quite happily for five years or more.

The total vineyards cover 1200 hectares (3000 acres) and produce about five million bottles each year. Eighty-five per-cent of the total is ordinary Montravel blanc. Apart from the six co-ops in the region the main vineyard owner is Domaine de Libarde, whose proprietor is Jean Claude Banizette of Nastringues. It is very small, just four hectares, and visitors are rarely permitted. See also Domaine du Gouyat at St Méard-de-Gurçon on the D708. Owned by Dudard Frères, visits are possible daily, tel. 53-82-45-26; Château de Montaigne at St Michel de Montaigne, tel. 53-58-60-56; Château de Masburel owned by Roland Barthoux at Fouqueyrolles. Visits by appointment, tel. 57-46-15-78; Château La Cabanelle at Golse-Pontchapt; and Domaine du Denoix at Le Denoix near Montcaret. Two of the top quality vineyards are Château Puy-Servain owned by M. Paul Hecquet at Cantalouette, near Pontchapt north of Port-St-Foy. Visits by appointment, tel. 57-46-11-46. Also, Château La Raye owned by Iteay de Peironin near Velines, tel. 53-27-50-14.

The Montravel vintage years of note were 1975, 1976, 1979, 1982, 1985 and 1986. The wines have a minimum of 12 degrees of alcohol and resemble the better premières Côtes de Bordeaux. The Montravel area is only 10 km east of the famous Saint-Emilion.

While you are in the small compact area be sure to visit the main sights. The superb Château de Montaigne is where the writer was born in 1533 and died in 1592. The sixteenth-century library is housed in a tower with a chapel, and has painted Latin and Greek texts ascribed to Michel Eyquem de Montaigne himself. The Romanesque church in the village is classified as **M.H.** Michel's brother lived at the Château de Mathecoulon in Montpeyroux a few km north. The twelfth-century Romanesque church has over 100 sculpted ornaments. Montcaret, just north of the D936, has a Roman villa with superb mosaics, a marvellous eleventh-century Romanesque church and a good small Gallo-Roman museum. Lamothe-Montravel (pop. 900) has another Montravel co-op, and was once the chief town of the 19 Montravel parishes. Spare a thought for the wretched English General Talbot, whose monument is a few km west of the town. On his death, defeat came to his army and the English had lost the Hundred Years War. Saint-Antoine-de-Breuilh (pop. 1500) is also on the D936, close to the river Dordogne, and has Montravel vineyards.

● **North eastern tour**

The main objective is to see the Pécharmant wine area. The wine is a brilliant red ruby colour with lots of body, well-rounded, and it ages well. The area is small, only 260 hectares, and grows between 8-10,000 hectolitres a year. It is a blend of Merlot (30%), Malbec (10%), Cabernet Franc (20%), and Cabernet Sauvignon (40%) grapes. The growers call it 'le vin de garde du Périgord'. It should be kept for three to six years in bottle. The best vintage years were 1975, 1976, and 1982, and 1985 looks very promising. Minimum alcohol is 11 degrees. Look out for Pécharmant.

Travel east from Bergerac on the river road D660 until you reach Creysse (pop. 1800) which has eight Paleolithic and Neolithic finds and digs, as well as a liqueur distillery. Lembras (pop. 750) and Saint Sauveur (pop. 450) are the two other Pécharmant villages a few km inland.

The main Pécharmant châteaux are as follows:
Château Champarel run by Mme Bouche; Château de Corbiac, tel. 53-57-20-70; Grand-Jaure run by M. Georges Baudry at Jaure, tel. 53-57-35-65; Domaine du Haut-Pécharmant run by Mme Reine Roches, tel. 53-57-29-50; Clos Peyrelevade run by Mme. Edith Girardet; Château de Tiregand owned by the Saint-Exupéry family near Creysse, tel. 53-23-21-08; and Domaine du Vieux Sapin, tel. 53-57-16-27 owned by the Cave Co-operative de Bergerac, which makes several estate wines. The largest producer is the Château de Tiregand which makes 175,000 bottles each vintage. The best château is Champarel, followed by La Renaudie, Peyrelevade and Corbiac.

While you are in the Pécharmant area do visit the Château of Montastruc close to Lamonzie-Montastruc on the D21 north of St Sauveur. It is one of the earliest English castles standing proudly on a hill (rebuilt in 1475).

In the UK Sookias and Bertaut, and Tanners import the Château de Tiregand 1985 wine, described as 'the most sophisticated of all Bergeracs, aged in oak for two years'. Haynes Hanson and Clark import Pécharmant wines from the Château of Grand Jaure, and Eldridge Pope from SODICOP, the co-operative of co-operatives. Recently I visited the co-op in Bergerac, Bd. de l'Entrepôt, tel. 53-57-16-27 and purchased a mixed case of vintage Pécharmant and Bergerac rouge which I have laid down for drinking in three or four years, time. The recent taxpaid price for the 1985 vintage Domaine

Brisseau Belloc, and Domaine du Vieux Sapin was 27.60 francs each.

Rosette is a mini-A.O.C. semi-sweet white wine grown north of Bergerac, with Sémillon, Sauvignon and Muscadelle grapes. Only 20,000 bottles are produced a year, and most is drunk locally. The limestone-clay soil produces a distinctive wine. Bernard Frères at Château Puypezat, Rosette, tel. 53-57-27-69 will welcome a visit. Rosette is also grown near Prigonrieux south of La Force, and at Lembras northeast of Bergerac.

● South eastern tour

This tour from Bergerac starts by heading to Monbazillac country via the N21. The wine is named locally *'L'Or du Périgord'*, the gold of Périgord. The area of 2500 hectares (6250 acres) is spread over five communes. Monbazillac itself (pop. 800) is well worth visiting. The sixteenth-century château is in excellent shape, with towers, wells and a park set in 20 hectares. It is one of the most elegant in the Dordogne. The local museum concentrates on the Protestant faith **and** on wine! It is owned by the Cave Co-operative who make nearly 30% of the total production of 50,000 hl. of wine (equal 8 million bottles).

The other communes are little Colombier (pop. 200) which has a twelfth-century Romanesque church and winetasting facilities, and Pomport (pop. 700) whose wines were known in the fifteenth century. *'Vins biologiques'* can be tasted here. St Laurent des Vignes (pop. 530) has a co-op and is sited on the old eleventh-century pilgrim route to St Jacques de Compostella in Spain. Finally, Rouffignac de Sigoulès (pop. 300) in the valley of the river Gardonnette. The five villages are close to each other and this wine tour would take a day depending on the number of stops.

The grape varieties are le Sémillon, Sauvignon and Muscadelle and the best vintages are 1978, 1980 and 1982, with those of 1985 and 1986 showing great promise. In the past the wine has been rather disappointing but recently the wine makers have been making much more effort. It now contains less sulphur and is cleaner. It can be drunk young, straw-gold in colour, sappy with the aroma of over-ripe grapes (the noble rot again). Conversely it can be kept for up to fifteen years as a rich *'vin liquoreux'* of great style. It has to be a minimum of 13% alcohol and is often more, so it may taste a little like a golden liqueur. The Dutch and Belgians take more Monbazillac than any other country.

The three best châteaux are Treuil de Nailhac owned by Vidal-Hurmic at Monbazillac, tel. 53-57-00-36; Repaire du Haut-Theulet run by Mme Bardan, tel. 53-58-30-30; and Abbaye de Saint-Mayne at Pomport, tel. 53-57-05-01. Next come Château la Borderie run by Dominique Vidal, Château Grand Chemin-Belingard, Château Le Fage, and finally Château de Sanxet, Château Les Olivoux, Château Ladesvignes, Château Haute-Fonrousse and Domaine du Haut-Montlong. The largest producer is the co-op which I recommend you visit first. Most château visits are by appointment only, except Château Treuil de Nailhac and Château Le Fage, both of which expect visitors and are quality houses. The small Repaire du Haute-Theulet also welcomes all visitors warmly. Just west of Colombier (see the wine Domaine de l'Ancienne Curé) is the magnificent sixteenth-century Château de Bridoire near the village of Ribagnac. Bridoire is not a wine château, but it is well worth a visit to see its towers, ramparts, chapel and moat.

After the co-op the largest wine producers are Château Haute-Fonrousse and Château Le Fage with about 70,000 bottles per annum, and Haute-Montlong and Les Olivoux with about 50,000 bottles each year. This gorgeous sweet yellow wine is imported by La Vigneronne of London (Clos Fontindoule), by Eldridge Pope, by Sookias and Bertaut (Château du Treuil de Nailhac), by the Hungerford Wine Company (Monbazillac co-op). Expect to pay between £4 and £5 per bottle. Of the Treuil de Nailhac 'Which?' Wine magazine says *'light and lemony . . . touch of botrytis, with honey and flowers in the taste'.*

● **South western tour**

The object of this tour is to see the small Saussignac appellation. The area produces 2,500 hls of a sweet white wine made from Sémillon grapes, halfway between the Côtes de Bergerac Moëlleux to the west and Monbazillac to the east. The alcoholic strength is between 12° and 15° and the French drink Saussignac as a slightly chilled apéritif, but then they like sweet apéritifs.

In the triangle southeast of Bergerac formed by the river Dordogne, the D935 for Marmande and the western department boundary, there are several important wine villages. Pomport has just been mentioned as a Monbazillac production area. Three-and-a-half km south is Sigoulès (pop. 600), a village perched on a hill, where there is a wine fair on the third Sunday in July. The major wine co-op is in the hamlet of Mescoules beside the D935. Contact M. Philippe Deschard, tel. 53-58-40-18. They produce all four Bergerac appellations – well worth a visit.

The best Saussignac vineyard is Château Court-les-Muts, run by young Pierre Sadoux at Razac de Saussignac, tel. 53-27-91-17, who welcomes visits. Bibendum of London describe him as *'an excellent grower, textbook winemaking ensures quality'*. The white Saussignac is a blend of 70% Sémillon and 30% Sauvignon grapes. The high proportion of Sémillon gives richness and complexity. M. Sadoux also produces excellent red, rosé and white Bergerac wines including the 1985 vintage. The 1984 red is aged in oak barrels. Usually he makes 5000 bottles a year of sparkling Blanc de Blancs *'Vin de Fête'*. It is made with the Ugni grape in true Champagne fashion with a minimum of two years age. Another good quality grower is M. Jean Gazziola who owns Château les Plaquettes at Saussignac. Visits by appointment, tel. 53-27-93-17. He has won many prizes for his red wines.

Other wine châteaux and domaines in this sector are:

Domaine des Comberies at Singleyrac, near Eymet, tel. 53-58-80-19. It is owned by M. Jean-Paul L'Homme and visits are possible daily.

Clos La Croix-Blanche owned by M. Michel Brouilleau at Monestier, 3 km west of Sigoulès, tel. 53-58-45-82, daily visits possible.

Domaine de Fraysse owned by M. Marcel Murer near Eymet, visits possible, tel. 53-23-81-38.

Château de Panisseau dates from the thirteenth century and is owned by M. Becker. At Thenac 3 km west of Sigoulès, tel. 53-58-40-03.

Château de Sanxet at Pomport is owned by M. de Passemar, tel. 53-58-37-46. Their white wine is served by the Norwegian Royal Family.

Château les Olivoux at Pomport, owned by M. Jean Dailliat, tel. 53-58-41-94, makes a typical modern Monbazillac wine.

Château Ladesvignes at Pomport, owned by Edmond Carrère, tel. 53-58-30-67 produces Monbazillac.

Domaine du Haut-Montlong at Pomport owned by M. Sergenton, tel. 53-58-44-88 produces Monbazillac.

Château Haute-Fonrousse near Sigoulès is owned by Serge Geraud, tel. 53-58-30-28.

Domaine de la Grange-Neuve at Pomport is owned by M. Castaing, tel. 53-58-42-23.

Issigeac (pop. 700) is a wine village on the D14 southeast of Monbazillac and there are several wine châteaux nearby. Moulin de Boisse owned by Jean-Louis Molle, allows visits, tel. 53-58-71-18; Château le Paradis owned by Roger Chambaut is at St Perdoux on the N21, tel. 53-58-36-69.

Henry Ryman, an Englishman using Australian wine production methods, bought the Château La Jaubertie near Colombier in 1973. Lay and Wheeler sell the wine in the UK for about £4. The white 1986 was described as *'dry, clean, most attractive wine made with Sauvignon and Sémillon grape varieties. Château La Jaubertie is one of the finest estates in the region.'* Majestic Wine Warehouses describe the same wine more vividly: *'Elderflower and gooseberries. Delicious dry and packed with fruity flavours.'* 'Which?' Wine magazine describe Ryman's Bergeracs Rosé of 1987, *'bright pink brashly catty fresh on the palate, unlikely cepage 85% Merlot, 15% Cabernet Sauvignon, firm fruit, acidity relatively high, elegantly almondy.'* His Domaine de Grandchamp 1986 stocked by Selfridges for £4.50 was described by the same magazine as *'aromatic rich, the ripe fruit controlled by careful*

oaking though fruit salad overtones were noted!' Appoint-
ments to visit Mr Ryman can be made by phoning in advance,
tel. 53-58-32-11.

Wine Co-ops

They all offer tasting facilities and a wide range of wines from
which you can make up a mixed case of 6 or 12 bottles. Most
co-ops are shut on Sunday and Monday.

1. **Bergerac:** Cave Co-op, Boulevard de l'Entrepôt, near
   SNCF station, tel. 53-57-16-27. They 'own' Domaine du
   Vieux Sapin.

2. **Monbazillac:** Cave Co-op, BP2, Monbazillac, tel.
   53-57-06-38. Visits preferably by appointment, They 'own'
   Château La Renaudie wines.

3. **Monbazillac:** – UNIDOR, Route de Mont de Marsan,
   24200 Sigoulès, tel. 53-57-40-44.

4. **Sigoulès – Mescoules:** 24240 Cave Co-op, tel.
   53-58-40-18 sell the following châteaux wines. Red from
   Les Justices, Les Carbonnières, Les Vigonies, Les Nicots,
   Malvielle, Les Valentines and Domaine de Monboucher.
   Also La Grande Borie, La Pleyssade, Le Sablou, Le
   Peyret and Rudelle. This co-op has 350 members in 31
   communes and stocks 100,000 hectolitres.

5. **Villefranche de Lonchat:** 24610, tel. 53-80-77-37.

6. **St Vivien et Bonneville:** 24230 St Vivien de Vélines, tel.
   53-27-52-22.

7. **Lamothe Montravel:** 24230 Velines, tel. 53-58-60-16.

8. **Carsac et St Martin de Gurson:** 24610, tel.
   53-80-78-84.

9. **Le Fleix:** 24130 La Force, tel. 57-46-20-25.

Wherever I go in France I always call in to see the local wine
co-op. I admire immensely what they are doing so efficiently
on behalf of the small wine farmers. They are all now modern
and efficient and produce quality wines hygienically! In
Bergerac the wine co-ops produce 40% of the total production from 2300 vigneron families.

Back in the UK

Below is a list of some Bergerac wines you should be able to find in the UK. Prices and availability were corrrect when we went to press.

Champagne de Villages sell Réné Monbouche's Château Grand Conseil, Bergerac blanc sec, rosé and Côtes de Bergerac rouge.

Oddbins shops stock Comte de Virecourt A.C. Bergerac and Château Fayolle A.C. Bergerac – both red wines below £3.

Gateway Food chain stock Château de Vignerons, Bergerac 1986 for £1.99 a bottle.

Berry Bros and Rudd sell 1986 Château Les Valentines A.C. Bergerac, 'stylish claret-like red wines' for under £4.

ASDA Food chain sell Bergerac rouge n.v. Paul Barbe for a little over £2, 'straightforward Cabernet taste, stalky and green'.

Bordeaux Direct have a Blanc de Blancs 1985 Cave St Laurent for about £3.

My personal advice would be to start with one or two bottles from Oddbins, decide the style you like, and then buy a mixed case from Sookias and Bertaut who specialise in good honest wines from the southwest of France. They are at The Cottage, Cambalt Rd, Putney Hill, London SW15 6EW, tel. 01-788-4193. They stock Château Court-les-Muts, Château du Tiregand and Château de Treuil de Nailhac – just about the best in the Bergerac region.

Another possibility is the Sunday Times Wine Club, who persuaded the Montravel Co-op of Cave St Vivien to allow an Australian winemaker to produce wines for them. The result is La Chapelle Sémillon A.O.C. Montravel white, Les Grisettes Merlot Bergerac rosé, and Le Clair des Haute Lieux Cabernet Sauvignon Bergerac rosé. Ask for the Flying Winemaker's case.

Visits

Various Wine Tour companies offer packaged wine tours to France including occasionaly to the Bergerac/Monbazillac region:

World Wine Tours (0865-891919); Blackheath Wine Trails (01-463-0012) and Arblaster and Clarke (0730-66883).

Allez France (09066-4279) has a vineyard visit scheme called Vinescapes which produces tailormade tours to your own specifications.

There are a dozen little distilleries producing *'eau de vie'* from apricots, pears, cherries, raspberries or bilberries — even from walnuts. They are often on sale at the many regional markets. Some are smooth, some are fiery — all at the same alcoholic strength as brandy or armagnac. They make an unusual present to bring back for the English winter.

CHAPTER THIRTEEN:
DELVING INTO PREHISTORY

The French study of prehistory began early in the nineteenth century. The original researchers concentrated on three areas – Périgord, Lozère and the valley of the Somme. Edouard Lartet studied the valley of the river Vézère and Gabriel de Mortillet various regions including the Dordogne. The former was greatly helped by two Englishmen: Henry Christy and Joseph Prestwich.

Palaeolithic and Neolithic

Over 200 sites with specific evidence of the evolution of man in the Palaeolithic age have been found in Périgord-Dordogne, and several have given their name to a human, type. The two key prehistoric eras were Palaeolithic (chipped stone implements 40-150,000 years ago) and Neolithic (polished stone implements 7,500 years ago).

The Neolithic era of 'homo sapiens' included three 'human' types. 'Chancelade' man was discovered from skeletons excavated in 1888 at Chancelade, a site 5 km northwest of Périgueux. The mongoloid cranium was considered to be pure Eskimo. Next came 'Cro-Magnon' man from a cave discovered in 1868 between Tayac and Les Eyzies de Tayac. Three skeletons, flints and bones were studied by Paul Broca who founded the School of Anthropology in France in the mid nineteenth century, and the race was so-called after the name of the local cave. The tall, strongly-formed bone structure was similar to the African Berber tribes. The last example of 'homo sapiens' was 'Grimaldi' man discovered in the south of France near Monaco, a smaller type similar to modern Bushmen and Hottentots.

The Palaeolithic period covers prehistory 40-150,000 years back to the age of the mammoth. 'Mousterian' man was discovered in 1909 at Le Moustier or Peyzac-le-Moustier, a hamlet on the west side of the river Vézère halfway between Les Eyzies and Montignac. At the same time *'La Ferrassie'* man (near Savignac de Miremont) was discovered, and also *'La Madeleine'* man near Tursac. These skeletal types were in the Neanderthal group (the Neander valley is near Düsseldorf), with strongly developed jawbones and stature just over five feet. Neanderthal man lived mainly in Africa about 150,000 years ago. Apart from the three Dordogne finds, another was made at La Chapelle-aux-Saints in the Corrèze.

The names frequently used now are *'Tayacian'* from Les Eyzies de Tayac, *'Mousterian'*, *'Magdalenian'*, *'Micoquean'* (La Micoque site is just north of Tayac, on the west side of the river Vézère), and finally *'Périgordian'* man'.

Bones and skeletons were of key importance to the anthropologists, but prehistory man's way of life is much more intriguing to the modern-day visitor to the Dordogne. Troglodytes, i.e. prehistoric cave-dwellers, lived in scores of underground villages or *abris* (shelters) mainly along the sides of the valley of the river Vézère. Their domestic tools and pottery, hunting weapons (flint blades and arrows), their personal ornaments (bracelets, ivory necklaces, shells, beads and other decorative vanities) and above all their art culture (wall paintings and engravings) are essential viewing for anyone visiting the region.

My advice is to start with a session at the Musée Nationale de Préhistoire clinging to the cliffs at Les Eyzies (pop. 900) in the eleventh-century castle owned by the barons of Beynac. It is open all the year except Tuesdays, tel. 53-06-97-03. This is the best prehistory museum, but there are others at Brantôme (Musée Desmoulin, open 1st April – 30th September, closed Tuesdays, tel. 53-05-70-21), at Beynac, open 15th June-15th September, at Sergeac (Musée de Castelmterle), at Peyzac-le-Moustier, open 2nd July – 31st August, tel. 53-04-86-21, at the Mairie at Tamnies, and at Le Thot in Thonac, closed Mondays, tel. 53-53-44-35. The Musée du Périgord in Périgueux has an excellent prehistoric collection in the Cours Tourny, tel. 53-53-16-42. The Société Historique et Archologique du Périgord, founded in 1874, is based in Périgueux.

Cracking the code

Some of the key words that will crop up in the search for prehistorical sites are:

Abris	underground rock shelter
Borie	dry stone beehive-shape shelter (for shepherds etc)
Cluzeau	underground refuge 'amenagé' i.e. furnished, arranged
Cristallisation	crystal stalactite or stalagmite
Dolmen	two large vertical stones with a third on top, usually marking a megalithic tomb
Gisement	stratified deposit
Grotte	cave
Site	setting or archeological 'dig' site
Fouilles	cut-out rock or earth 'stratas' or digs
Gouffre/Igue/Aven	vertical shaft or large hole in rocks
Cloup/Sotch	as above
Megalith	large upright boulder or stone, sometimes part of a dolmen
Sousterrains	underground sites
Spéléologie	pot-holing
Refuge	refuge or shelter, see Abris
Neolithique	neolithic, later Stone Age period
Trou prehistorique	see Cluzeau
Troglodyte	troglodyte — early man who lived in rock/cliff faces
Polissoir	polished stone implement (tool or weapon) of Neolithic age

Prehistoric objects of worship

In many parts of the Dordogne you can see the evidence of prehistoric man emerging from the subterranean depths as the world grew warmer, probably between the Neolithic era of 7500 BC and the Bronze Age of 2500 BC. He then built above ground little drystone 'beehive' shaped shelters close to the caves. Over the centuries many of these 'bories' have been preserved and since used by shepherds. When we lived in the Lot department (the next one south bordering the Dordogne) we had a perfect 'borie' on our land, about 10 feet tall, vaulted, with a diameter of about eight to nine feet. The stones were beautifully shaped and tiered so the inside was rain- and wind-free and very snug.

I have located some small villages in the Dordogne with these strange stone shelters, dating probably from about 2000 BC. East of Périgueux at Limeyrat is a 'borie', dolmen and tumulus, and another group at Chourgnac of 'cabanes en pierre dites bories'. At Florimont-Gaumier (pop. 230) 12 km south of Domme on the minor road to the hamlet of Boulegan is a delightful 'hutte de pierres seches coiffée en pain de sucre'. Badefols-sur-Dordogne nearby has a dozen 'beehive' shelters of dry stone.

Saint André d'Allas (pop. 350) is a village 5 km west of Sarlat, and nearby at the site of Breuil is a group of traditional Neolithic 'cabanes voutées de coupoles en encorbellement'. It is a classified site close to the prehistoric grotto of Roch and 'abri' under the Pas-Estre rocks. A few km south is Vézac (pop. 450) which has a hamlet of dry stone bories on the hillside near the classified château of Marqueysac.

A few km west of Excideuil, 30 km northeast of Périgueux, is the village of St Germain-des-Prés (pop. 650) which has a series of 'bories', one being at La Moranchie. Sorges (pop. 900) is a few km to the west and is known for its truffles, dog fairs, summer art exhibition and a village of dry stone 'bories'. Antonne-et-Tregonant (pop. 1000) between Sorges and Périgueux has rocks with cupolas of Borie-Belet, near the splendid fifteenth-century Château des Bories. Many prehistoric funeral urns were discovered at Jumilhac-le-Grand northeast of Thiviers. At Rouffignac-le-Sigoulès (pop. 260), just west of Monbazillac, is the funeral grotto of Fontanguillère, and there is another at Coux et Bigaroque.

The Dordogne has its equivalent to Stonehenge, but not on such a grand scale. Huge upright stones, probably with a funereal or religious purpose, can be found across the Dordogne. Menhirs are tall vertical prehistoric monumental stones taking their name from the Breton *'men hir'* (stone, long). A megalith is the same, but might be larger than a menhir, and a dolmen consists of two megalithic stones with an equally large stone laid across the top, possibly deriving from the Cornish Celt word *'tolmen'* (hole of stone). Stonehenge is made up of a vast range of dolmens. In the Dordogne the local vernacular called dolmens, menhirs or megaliths *'pierres levées'*, or erected, lifted up stones. They usually marked the site of Neolithic burial chambers.

At Javerlhac, northwest of Nontron, is a prehistoric sacrificial altar called *'La Pierre Virande'*, which shows an alternative usage! I have located over a hundred sites of dolmens, menhirs and megaliths, and have selected a score for visitors interested in archeology, in regional clusters. If in **bold** type it infers a site of note.

The main dolmen area is southeast of Bergerac and east of Issigeac. Baneuil, Beaumont (**du Blanc**), Sainte Sabine (Roc de Gause), Saint Léon-d'Issigeac (Brel and Roc de la Chevre). Then a little further east Belvès (two, several menhirs and a polissoir), Vergt-de-Biron (Point-du-Jour), Rampieux (**Peyrelevade**), Marsales (l'Oustal du Loup), Saint-Cassien (la Courrège and Neolithic polissoir des Charrieux), Saint-Chamassy (Cantagrel). Further east again, Siorac-en-Périgord (Cayrelevat), Saint-Pardoux-et-Vielvic (Bonarme and a polissoir), St Amand-de-Belves (Langlade), Domme (**Giverzac**), Vitrac (La Pierre au Diable and **Peyrelevade**) and Saint Laurent-la-Vallée (Peyrelongue).

Northwest of Bergerac there are two sites; Saint-Méard-de-Gurcon (Peyre Plantade) and Villamblard (Peyrelevade shaped like a table). Near Périgueux are St Aquiln (**Peyrebrune**), Tocane-Saint-Apre (Margot), and **Beauregard et Bassac**, a small English *bastide* village.

East of Périgueux, at Ajat, Limeyrat (Peyrelevade), and at Terrasson-la-Villedieu, there are several dolmens.

North of Périgueux dolmens are to be seen at Paussac-et-Saint Vivien (**Peyre d'Ermale** and **Peyrelevade**), at Valeuil (**Laprouges** and megalith of **des Coutoux**), at Brantôme (**'La Pierre Levée'**) and Condat sur Trincou (**Peyre-Levade**).

Northeast of Périgueux at Thiviers (Pierrefiche), at Saint-Jory-de-Chalais (Pierre-Levée) and Payzac (La Morelie). Finally near Nontron at Saint-Estèphe is the menhir of Fixard, and further north another at Saint Bartholemy de Bussière.

Quite a few menhirs, dolmens and megaliths have local names connected with the Devil i.e. objects of superstition and dread!

Troglodytes

Before prehistoric man came out of the caves, he and his mate usually lived in troglodyte villages in the cliff-faces such as La Madeleine near Tursac, tel. 53-53-44-35, closed Tuesday out of season and December-February, and La Roque Saint-Christophe at Le Moustier, tel. 53-50-70-45, open 15th March to 15th November. Man came out of his below ground caves, grottos and 'abri' shelters after the Magdalenian era about 8000 BC .

The Tursac area is rich in troglodyte shelters, and seven out of the score are *'sites classés'* such at Liveyre, *'Abri Cellier'*, La Forêt, Ruth, Roque Barbel, La Madeleine, and the strongpoint (early fort) of Reignac, Pas du Miroir 8 km distant was another troglodyte village, where stone lamps have been found.

Further southwest down the valley of the river Vézère there are troglodyte *'habitations'* to be found in Couze-et-Saint Front opposite Lalinde. Just west is Mouleydier with troglodyte dwellings at St Cybard. Southeast of Sarlat in the Dordogne river valley is St Julien de Lampon, where underneath the holy fountain of devotion of St Julien is a troglodyte refuge called 'Saint-Mondane'. To the southeast near Belvès in the hamlet of Larzac is a *'grotto-cluzeau'* with the curious name *'des Anglais'* with troglodyte graffiti. Perhaps it was discovered by English archeologists in the nineteenth century?

Southwest from Nontron in the small village of La Rochebeaucourt-et-Argentine is the troglodyte fort of Argentine among the numerous stone quarries. As 'homo sapiens' became bolder, the occasional stone fort was made into a prehistoric encampment. Southwest of Riberac is the village of Saint-Privat which has such a camp.

Near Lanouaille in the northeast of the department is the village of Dussac with a prehistoric encampment called Castel-Sarrazi. One of the strangest sites of all is at Caudon on the river Dordogne south bank opposite the château of Montfort, which has a troglodyte **church** with bell tower and bells constructed in a rockface cave.

The Neolithic Age, part of the Stone Age, was about 5000-7000 BC and was also known as the era of polished stone tools and weapons, or in French 'Polissoir'.

In a few villages in the Dordogne there have been discoveries of various polished stone implements. At Belvès, Carves (west of Domme), Festalemps (west of Riberac), Mauzens-et-Miremont (northwest of Les Eyzies), where the Neolithic *polissoir* is called 'Pierre des Justices', Monsac (south of Lalinde), Orliaquet (east of Sarlat), the *polissoir* called 'des Charrieux' at Saint Cassien (near Monpazier). There are more at Saint-Cyprien (west of Sarlat), Saint Léon-d'Issigeac (east of Issigeac), Saint Pardoux-et-Vielvic (near Belvès) and at Thenon (east of Périgueux), once called Jarripigier. Many of the original *polissoir* implements can now be seen in the major prehistory museums of the Dordogne.

Planning your visits

With over 200 sites to visit it is not an easy choice for tourists with a relatively short time available. The Caisse Nationale des Monuments Historiques et des Sites, 48 rue Gambetta, Périgueux, tel. 53-08-41-56, organises guided tours between June and September of all the main prehistoric sites, with a commentary in French and English.

One or more of the museums at Périgueux, Les Eyzies, Thonac/Thot, Beynac, Peyzac-le-Moustier, Brantôme and Eymet should be visited for a start. Then a look at one of the troglodyte villages of La Madeleine (Tursac) or La Roque

Saint-Christophe at Le Mustier. Next one or more of the major *gisements*, *grottes* or *abris ornes* (furbished dwelling shelters).

What I have tried to do is to produce two tables — one of really important sites organised for visitors — and a second table of important sites, which remain '*au naturel*'. Most of these are clustered together along the small hills overlooking the river Vézère, easily reached from Sarlat.

The famous **Grotto of Lascaux** was discovered on 12th September 1940 by four lads searching for a lost dog. The site and cavern is 2½ km south of Montignac (pop. 3100). Luckily the boys, having discovered the four large underground caves with their incredible paintings created about 15,000 years ago, had enough sense to tell their schoolmaster. He in turn, equally sensibly, prevailed on the national expert on Palaeolithic are, Abbé Breuil to come and look at it. Huge white bulls, black bulls, Chinese horses, bison, deer and ibex in a wide range of exciting colours were depicted on the cave surfaces. Breuil and the other experts decreed that Lascaux was the greatest collection of prehistoric art in the world. In the next 23 years millions of startled visitors made the pilgrimage to this extraordinary find entitled '*La Chapelle Six-tine de la Préhistoire*'. Sadly the paintings rapidly deteriorated after continual exposure to carbon dioxide and, as a result Lascaux I has been closed. Lascaux II has arisen — a meticulous modern reconstruction which should be visited. It is closed in January and on Mondays out of season, tel. 53-53-44-35. Tickets are on sale in Montignac under the arcades or at the well-signed site on the hillside for hourly visits from 9.30 a.m. in season (Jul/Aug) and 10 a.m. out of season. About 40 francs for Lascaux II and Le Thot.

Since there were no domestic tools, weapons or bones found, the implication is that the Lascaux caves were dedicated to a pagan faith based on fertility (pregnant female animals) and hunting (animals pierced by arrows or painted in a primitive trap). Quite a few grottos/abris/shelters have had curious names handed down over the years, such as '*sorcier*' (magician or sorcerer) and '*enfer*' (hell).

Near Lascaux and Montignac is the grotto of **Régourdou** discovered in 1954, which dates from the Mousterian era, much older than Lascaux, where Neanderthal man lived and fought bears whose skeletons were found here, tel. 53-51-81-23. It is closed from December to February. A third classified site nearby is that of **La Balutie**.

From Montignac southwest to Les Eyzies on the D706 and D65 are scores of classified prehistoric sites. The most important are in **bold** type.

Le Thot 4 km before Thonac, has Paleolithic sites at Maillot and Losse, and Neolithic around Losse. A modern building contains the prehistoric museum with sorcerer's well, tel. 53-53-44-35 (same hours as Lascaux) and animal park with live wild boar, bison, taipan horses and stags.

Sergeac (pop. 140) is 2½ km further down the road. Discoveries were made in 1880 of the classified sites of Blanchard, Labattut, **Reverdit**, Castanet and several others. It is a pretty hamlet with fortified twelfth-century Romanesque church, grey slated houses, a Templar *'commanderie'* and an attractive sixteenth-century stone cross at the crossroads. There is a small prehistory museum at Castel-merle.

Castelmerle has a shelter with cave sculptures of the upper Paleolithic era 10,000 years ago, tel. 53-50-77-76. Closed Wednesday and October − March.

Peyzac-le-Moustier (pop. 120) gave its name to the Mousterian Age of the middle Paleolithic period. A German archeologist discovered a prehistoric Neanderthal-type skeleton here during a dig in 1908. The site is on the west bank near the D706, tel 53-06-92-90. It is open from 15th May to 15th September, but only two days a week. Ask at the Auberge de Vimont nearby. On the eastern bank is the rock-cliff troglodyte village of La Roque St Christophe which is 80 metres high and 800 metres in length. Three thousand Neanderthal men lived here 50,000 years ago, with traces of their tools, daily life, art and culture. Later on persecuted Christians came here for shelter, an engraving of a fish, one of their signs, and a fine 'Madonna' engraving have been found. It was occupied in turn by both sides in the Hundred Years War and later by hunted Huguenots, tel. 53-50-70-45. Entry 20 francs.

For 3½ km the D65 follows the curve of the river to **Tursac** (pop. 240) which is one of the top four prehistoric sites in the

Dordogne. In 1863 the *'abri'* under the rockface, called La Madeleine, was explored by Edouard Lartet and Christy. The *'gisement'* is in the bend of the river on the west side near the castle of La Goudelie. The troglodyte village of La Madeleine gave its name to the Magdalenian culture of the upper Paleolithic era when bone/ivory carvings from reindeer produced necklaces, arrows and harpoons. Listed sites here include Liveyre, 'Abri Cellier', La Forêt, Le Ruth (tel. 53-50-74-01, the Pages collection), Roque Barbel and the troglodyte stronghold of Reignac. Most of the finds have been removed to the prehistory museum in Sarlat. Visits may be made to La Madeleine, tel. 53-53-44-35. It is closed from December to February and Tuesdays out of high season.

Keep on the D706 for another 6 km to **Les Eyzies-de-Tayac** (pop. 900) which, as a prehistoric area, has been given the title of 'capital of prehistory', and which gave its name to the Tayacian period when mammoths and elephants roamed the region up to 150,000 years ago! The small town is sited where the river Beune flows from the east into the Vézère. Within half a day it is possible to visit most of the 20 classified sites, although a visit to the museum first is recommended.

Appropriately for strong walkers the Grande Randonnée routes GR 6, 36 and 64 all pass west-east through Les Eyzies.

On the east side of the Vézère is the prehistoric museum, Grotto of **Font-de-Gaume**, des **Combarelles**, **La Mouthe**, **Cro-Magnon**, then east along the D48 and the river Beune is Laussel (and château), **Cap Blanc** and the château of Commarque.

On the west side of the Vézère is the museum of La Spéléologie, the gorge d'Enfer, **abri du Poisson**, **Grotto du Grand Roc**, La Laugerie (basse and haute), **Carpe-Diem** (200m metres long with fine stalactites) and La Micoque.

First explorations started in 1868 and have continued ever since. So important were the finds of skeletons, tombs, paintings, bone implements and adornments that the area gave its name not only to the Tayacian period, but also to Cro-Magnon Man and Micoquean (La Micoque).

● **Chief sites**
1. **Font de Gaume Cave**, tel. 53-08-00-94. Open all the

year except Tuesdays and 25th November – 25th December. See the frescoes, marvellous coloured paintings of bison, mammoths, reindeer and black horses. Two hundred have been catalogued, including 23 mammoths!

2. **Les Combarelles Cave**, tel. 53-08-00-94. Open all the year except Wednesdays, and most of March. Discovered in 1901, the 300 metres of passageway are covered with works of art. Look for the rock engravings of a reindeer and 300 animal drawings.

3. **Grand Roc Grotto**, tel. 53-06-96-76. Open 18th March – 15th November. Here is a display of what the French call '*cristallisations*' of stalactites, stalagmites and a wide variety of pendants, resulting from an underground river.

4. **Laugerie Haute**, tel. 53-08-00-94. Open all the year. Closed on Tuesdays. A wide range of prehistoric tools, weapons, adornments and several skeletons in a small museum show convincingly prehistoric man's lifestyle for a period of 20,000 years.

5. **Laugerie Basse**, tel. 53-06-97-12. The site called Les Marseilles revealed a collection of implements, needles and tools.

6 **Carpe Diem**, tel. 53-06-93-63, is just west of the Laugeries on the D31 out of Manaurie village. The grotto is open for tours from April to the end of September. There are many coloured stalactites and stalagmites.

7. **Abri de Cap Blanc**, tel. 53-59-12-74, is at Marquay 12½ km east of Les Eyzies on the D47/D48. Closed November-March. In 1909 sculpture and rock carvings of bison and horses were discovered, as well as a human grave.

Other important sites are the Grotto of **La Mouthe**, closed on Mondays, discovered in 1895. You go along a narrow passage for 100 metres to see many ochre drawings of prehistoric animals, a lantern and drawing of a prehistoric hut; **Abri Cro-Magnon** discovered in 1868 where the skeletons found gave their name to that prehistoric man, in the Upper

Paleolithic period; **Abri du Poisson** where you see the metre-long salmon carved on the cave roof; and finally the **Gorge d'Enfer** where you can talk to the real animals, related to those portrayed in the many caves!

Now you need to make a detour 10 km northwest of Les Eyzies by the D47 into the hinterland, but for a good cause. **The Grotte de Rouffignac**, also known as Cro-de-Granville, or Miremont, is one of the four top prehistoric sites in the Dordogne. Professor Nougier in 1956 discovered a collection of wall engravings and paintings of rhinocerous, horses, ibex and battles between mammoths, as well as stags rutting. Oddly enough the 8 km of galleries and chambers had been known by the local peasantry since the fifteenth century. Before the Wehrmacht destroyed the village in March 1944, their more cultured members must have visited the caves – a well-known curiosity. Now known officially as the Grotte aux Cents Mammouths, the tour of 4 km is made by electric train, tel. 53-05-41-71. Closed November to Easter.

Southwest of Les Eyzies for 7 km along the D706 we come to **Le Bugue** (pop. 3000) which has two significant sites. The cave of Bara-Bahau, tel. 53-07-28-82, is closed from 1st November to the end of March. Discovered as recently as 1951, the hundred metre long cave has many flint engravings of rhinocerous, oxen, horses and bison with curious human finger marks. On the east side of the river Vézère is the Gouffre (chasm) de Proumeyssac, tel. 53-07-27-47, which is closed from December to mid January. Go via the D31 signed for Audrix. It is one of the best collections of *'cristallisations'* in the Dordogne.

Halfway between Les Eyzies and Le Bugue on the west bank of the river is **Saint-Cirq du Bugue** (pop. 120) which has the Grotto du Sorcier with painting of the 'magician' and a small museum, tel. 53-07-14-37. It is open from Easter to the end of September. M. Lagrange will be your guide to see the *magdalenienne* engravings of animals at 'Sous-le Roc' site.

Southeast of Les Eyzies 7 km on the D47/48 is the **Grotto of Bernifal** near Meyrals (pop. 400). The site was discovered in 1902 and has many interesting paintings and engravings of animals and unusual patterns, tel. 53-29-66-39. Open July and August. Two other good reasons for making this detour are the triangular fifteenth-century Château de la Roque with its sixteenth century mural paintings in the oratory, and the 'best bread in France'! There are summer concerts in La Rougerie manor house.

Without doubt the Vézère valley is the ultimate in prehistoric finds, but for the keen amateur archeologist I have 'uncovered' further sites all over the Dordogne. If you are in the area, worth a **small** detour!

Site	Nearest Town	Comments
Villars (pop. 650) Tel. 53-54-82-36 Easter – end Sept.	Nontron – 15 km	Grotto Cluzeau (D82) Sorcier paintings, stalagmites. Painting of the blue horse
Teyjat (pop. 400) Tel. 53-56-31-62 Easter – end Sept.	Nontron – 10 km NW	Grotto de la Mairie, paintings, engravings, small museum
La Gonterie-Boulouneix (pop. 200) See Romanesque church	Nontron – 20 km SW	Abri de Tabaterie and Roc-Plat
Bayac (pop. 300) on river Couze	Lalinde – 4 km S	Gisemet of La Gravette and various grottos
Bourniquel (pop. 90) east of Bayac	Lalinde – 5 km S	Gisements of Champs-Blancs and Malpas
Tamnies (pop. 300)	Sarlat – 9 km NW	Exhibition of prehistory at Mairie
St Amand-de-Coly (pop. 300) (see abbey & château)	Sarlat – 25 km N	Six prehistoric gisements
Carsac-Aillac (pop. 800) on river Dordogne	Sarlat – 10 km S	Gisements of Pech-de-l'Aze and Pech-de-la Boissière

Site	Nearest Town	Comments
Domme (pop. 900) (See museum Paul Reclus for Paleolithic finds)	Sarlat – 14 km S	Abri of Combe-Grenal grottos of Jubile, Redoulou Troglodyte church at Caldon
Grolejac (pop. 500) See twelfth-century church	Sarlat – 16 km SE	Abri of La Gane, Grotto of Pechialet
St André d'Allas (pop. 350) See twelfth-century church	Sarlat – 5 km E	Grotto of Roche. Abri Pas-Estré Neolithic site of Breuil
La Chapelle-Faucher (pop. 500) See Château de Lasfond	Périgueux – 20 km N, on D3	Gisement of Rocheraille
Trelissac (pop. 6500)	Périgueux – 6 km E	Paleolithic site of Rodas. Neolithic of Jacots and La Croix-du-Duc
Chancelade (pop. 2500) See twelfth-century abbey	Périgueux – 6 km NW	Grotto of Raymonden. Skull of homo sapiens discovered 1888, named 'Chancelade man'
Excideuil (pop. 1900) See twelfth-century castle	Périgueux – 25 km NE	Grottos of St Martin
Grand-Brassac (pop. 600) See twelfth-century fortified church	Périgueux – 25 km NW	Gisement of Rochereuil

Site	Nearest Town	Comments
Saint-Astier (pop. 4000) See Puyferrat castle, eleventh-century church	Périgueux – 15 km SW	Neolithic sites at Batut, Crognac and Paypinson
Thenon (pop. 1250)	Périgueux – 20 km E	Seven prehistoric sites
Mauzens-et-Miremont (pop. 300)	Périgueux – 30 km SE	Gisement La Faurelie. Neolithic polissoir
Valeuil (pop. 300)	Périgueux – 20 km NW	Site of Chauterie; Dolmen; Megalith
Creysse (pop. 1800)	Bergerac – 8 km E	Eight Paleolithic gisements
Villamblard (pop. 850)	Bergerac – 20 km N	Seven Paleolithic sites
Queyssac (pop. 300)	Bergerac – 10 km NE	Three gisements, six cluzeaux
Lalinde (pop. 3100) See Château de Laffinoux	Bergerac – 25 km E	Four prehistoric cluzeaux
Monestier (pop. 350)	Bergerac – 20 km SW	Gisements of Font-Marty la Croix-Blanche, La Maisonette

Site	Nearest Town	Comments
Mussidan (pop. 3250)	Bergerac – 30 km NW	Three gisements
Sourzac (pop. 1000)	Mussidan – near	Grotto of Las Agnelas/Gaillou
Périgueux (pop. 35,000) See Musée du Périgord		Gisements of Petit-Puynousseau, Gour de l'Arche, Commeymies, Campriac, Le Toulon
Sagelat (pop. 250)	Belvès – 3 km	Five gisements
Terrasson-la-Villedieu (pop. 6200)	Sarlat – 35 km N	Grotto of St Sours Camp du Mas. Bronze age oppidum of La Roche-Liberé
Valojoulx (pop. 170)	Sarlat – 18 km NW	Site of La Combe, Delage Frasses and Costeperier
Vezac (pop. 420) See Château of Marqueyssac	Sarlat – 10 km SW	Grotto du Roc
Vitrac (pop. 620)	Sarlat – 10 km SW	Gisement of Madame de Gerard, many sites, dolmen

The final prehistory region lies eastwards along the river Dordogne into the Lot (Quercy) department, where there are five more sites of grottos and caves.

1. **Cougnac** just north of Gourdon with cave paintings and mineral crystallisations. tel. 65-41-06-11. Isolated but well worth a visit. Open from Easter to 1st November.

Then in a cluster 20 km east northeast are:

2. **Lacave** with a complex of 12 grottos visited by electric train, tel. 65-37-87-03.

3. **Padirac**, a natural wonder with many km of underground caverns and grottos reached by lift initially, and by boats, tel. 65-33-64-56. Open 25th March – mid October. Although it has no prehistoric remains it is one of the most entertaining visits for the family.

4. **Presque** with grotto *colonnes* (pillars), tel. 65-38-07-44 (near St Céré). Open 26th March – 8th October.

5. **The Grotto des Merveilles** at L'Hospitalet-Rocamadour at the top near the castle, tel. 65-33-67-92. Open Easter to 1st November.

Helpful hints

The caves can be cold and damp so warm clothes are advisable. Some passageways can be slippery and I would recommend strong walking shoes. In high season try to get to your selected site as early as possible to avoid crowds. Ask for an English-speaking guide if one is available.

You should expect to pay about 20-25 francs per person for guided tours. Out of season check by phone or ask the local information office for times of opening. Finally you might like to ponder why our prehistoric ancestors painted, drew or engraved every predatory animal known to them in great and convincing detail – but very, very rarely depicted 'homo sapiens'.

CHAPTER FOURTEEN:
CASTLES, CHURCHES AND
CULTURAL EVENTS

French castles and châteaux are amongst the most attractive and interesting buildings in the world. Although the Loire region probably has the most grand and elegant collection in France, the Dordogne wins on sheer numbers.

After the first glimpse of one of the twelve hundred châteaux in the Dordogne it is worth looking at it again with a historian's eye. Why was it built **here**? Was it to command and dominate a vital road or river? Was it built on a spur or hillside to protect a village or town nearby? If it was built about the thirteenth-century was it conceived by the English troops and architects of King Henry II and his French queen, or by Phillipe Le Bel, his opposite number, who sponsored scores of French castles? If it was an early-built castle was it moated and where was its vital spring-well source? A siege might take many months and water and stocks of food would be vital. How would you go about checking the defensive position? Is it overlooked for plunging arrows to harass your garrison? Are there copses nearby where the attacker can marshal his forces? Are the (remaining) walls or ramparts high and thick enough to withstand ladder attacks or even mining? The keep or *donjon* was the vital defensive building usually erected in the twelfth-century. Later owners might have added a fifteenth-century belfry, or extra high wings. If it was built in the seventeenth-century or even later it was probably for social and status reasons. The lovely slate-blue pepperpot towers, huge chimney pieces and Renaissance dormer windows will tell you a lot about its owners. Magnificent staircases and courts of honour inside were for balls and receptions.

Some of the best illustrations of the various styles to be seen: **Beynac**, captured by Richard Coeur de Lion is classic-aggressive style. **Château Montfort** is photographed by every traveller for its fairytale position high above the river

Dordogne. For the historian, **Biron** is one of the most fascinating. Over eight centuries each generation has added a different feature. **Hautefort** is the nearest in style to a grand château of the Loire, and **Jumilhac-le-Grand** is probably the most elegant and romantic. But there are still another 1000 to look at and assess — a photographer's dream. A pity you cannot capture the scene of which Bertrand de Born wrote and sang in 1190 as lord of Hautefort, *'And I love to see tents and pavilions dressed on the fields, and I am filled with happiness to see knights and lords in armour ranged in the countryside.'* That was before our King Henry II besieged Hautefort and captured Bertrand!

The enterprising tourist office of the Limousin has published a leaflet entitled 'La Route Richard Coeur de Lion' which ends at Jumilhac-le-Grand and La Coquille, châteaux in northern Périgord.

It is a wonder that so many castles have survived the ravages of war and of peace. In the fifteenth century during the Hundred Years War, the English destroyed the French castles, and vice versa. More were destroyed in the religious wars of the sixteenth century when Huguenots battled with Catholics. The brave citizens of the Revolution tore down castle walls in the cause of equality and so it went on. For instance the château of Clerans east of Bergerac was occupied alternately by French and English troops for 150 years. Nevertheless in the tourist season at least 30 castles are open to the public. Some have been beautifully restored, such as **Beynac**, others, such as the huge, grand edifice of Biron, continue to be repaired with funds from the state. Expect to pay about 20 francs for a ticket and guided tour — usually this cost is well worth while.

I have put the selected castles into clusters for convenient visiting on regional tours.

Nontron and the North

This town is the best base for castle-spotting in the northern sector of the Dordogne. There are a score or more châteaux within easy drive of **Nontron**, but eight are really stunning, set in beautiful villages.

The D75 runs northwest parallel to the railway and little

147

river Bandiat heading towards Angoulême. **Variagnes** (pop. 450) has a well preserved château, part thirteenth century, repaired in the sixteenth century, with a keep and square tower which usefully doubles up as a permanent exhibition of the local arts of spinning and weaving and nineteenth-century peasant lifestyle. Closed on Tuesday, tel. 53-56-35-76. Varaignes is 15 km from Nontron. The annual fair, Fête du Marende, on the first Sunday in August, takes place in the castle courtyard with '*repas périgourdin à l'ancienne*'.

There are four interesting listed castles to the east of Nontron. **Jumilhac-le-Grand** is well named. It is probably the most elegant château in the Dordogne, ranking with **Hautefort** (c.v.) As the crow flies it is about 50 km cross country (Michelin Map 72) or 25 km northeast from Thiviers on the D78. The small town of 1500 population was a Gallo-Roman site and the '*château fort*' was in being in the twelfth century. It was taken by the English troops and later rescued for the French by Du Guesclin. It stands grandly on the small river L'Isle and has a dozen grey slate steepled turrets, in pep-perpot style. For two centuries the castle was owned by the Knights Templars until in 1579 the Chapelle de Jumilhac family acquired it when the Templars were disgraced by the King. The main local industry was that of forges driven by water mills on the river l'Isle. Forged metal designs can be seen on the top of the turrets − the sun, the moon, angels, birds and a cupid. Most of the elegant fittings inside are fifteenth-century. (The original feudal chapel is next door.) The room of the spinning maiden 'La Fileuse', great chimneys, court of honour, balustraded terrace and flood-lighting during the summer evenings make Jumilhac a must, tel. 53-52-54-68. The summer season is 1st July to 15th September. From 15th March to 1st July and 15th September to 15th November it is open only on Sunday afternoons. Closed mid-winter.

La Marthonie dominated the village square of the pictures-que medieval village of Saint Jean de Côle (pop. 300) which is on the D707 10 km west of Thiviers. The English troops fortified the village 1394-1404. The château is mainly fifteenth-century, but the two main towers are fourteenth-century. Mondot de la Martonie rebuilt the castle in the sixteenth century and later a wing and fine staircase were added. Open to visitors in July and August, tel. 53-62-30-25. The Association 'Les amis du vieux St Jean' here helped make Saint Jean de Côle one of the prettiest and most interesting villages in the Dordogne. See also the twelfth-century abbey-church, with cloister, library and carvings and the Roman bridge over the river Côle.

Puyguilhem Château is on the north side of Villars (pop. 650) which is 30 km due south from Nontron and 20 km west of Thiviers on the D3 overlooking the river Trincou. The pilgrims passed this way en route to St Jaques de Compostella, although in 1342 the village was occupied by brigands. Early in the sixteenth century Mondot de la Marthonie, first president of the Bordeaux parliament, rebuilt the original château and it was completed by his son in 1530. The French nation restored it after World War II. The stairways, chimney breasts, attic windows and main towers are key features, tel. 53-53-44-35. Open all year, closed on Tuesdays. **Villars** should also be visited for its Cistercian abbey of Boschaud and prehistoric grottos (Cluzeau), stalactites and megalith. There is a summer exhibition of local *'artisanat'* work.

Les Bernardières is a château overlooking the river Nizonne, near Champeaux-et-la-Chapelle-Pommier (pop. 250), equidistant from Nontron and Mareil to the southwest. The French general Du Guesclin besieged the castle in 1377 but the English troops held out. A later owner called Antoine d'Authon was converted to Islam and became Pasha of Algiers. It really is a stronghold with moat, huge walls, thirteenth-century towers and fourteenth-century *'donjon'* or keep. One of the main gates in the ramparts is named after King Henri II. Formal gardens and terraces with balustrade stretch down to the Nizonne river, tel. 45-95-55-64. Closed Tuesday, open 1st July to mid-September. The neighbouring sixteenth-century **Château de Puycheny** is worth a look.

Richemont is in the village of Saint Crépin de Richemont on the north side of the D939 half way between Mareuil and Brantôme. The sixteenth-century château overlooking the river Boulou was built by the Abbot of Brantôme, who was more famous as an author called Pierre de Bourdeille. The

149

strong square tower, the two long wings of the château and its decorated chapel are of note, tel. 53-05-72-81. Closed Fridays, open 15th July to 31st August.

Bourdeilles is a picturesque village (pop. 650) dominating the river Dronne 10 km southwest of Brantôme. Parts of it date from the eleventh century. Geraud de Maumont rebuilt the château in the thirteenth century and a superb keep was constructed. It was often besieged; the English took it in 1369 and Du Guesclin retook it in 1377. Partly a feudal stronghold, it is also partly a Renaissance château. The Bourdeilles family were one of the four great baronies of Périgord who eventually offered the château to the French state. The latter has restored the buildings and organises concerts there amid a superb collection of antique furniture in the medieval hall. Open all the year except Tuesdays out of season, tel. 53-53-44-35. One of the most elegant châteaux in the Dordogne, it has a superb view from the terraces of the river Dronne, and is well worth a visit. We visited it recently on a Sunday. By chance that day entry was free and we climbed to the top of the keep to survey the countryside.

Mareuil sur Belle, (pop. 1200) is another of the four major Périgord baronies, situated near the river Belle 21 km south west of Nontron on the D708. A well established fortress in the twelfth century, it belonged to the family of Arnaud de Mareuil, born 1150, a noted troubadour. The English partly destroyed it in the fourteenth century and it was rebuilt in the sixteenth century by Guy de Mareuil, with a deep moat and drawbridge. The Talleyrand-Périgord family owned it for nearly three centuries but, in poor condition, it was sold to the Hospices de Chalais. Resold again in 1964 it has now been almost completely restored including the flamboyant Gothic-style chapel, and subterranean dungeons, tel. 53-60-91-35. Closed Wednesdays and in the winter months.

Périgueux

If you are based in Périgueux there are half a dozen notable châteaux within easy distance to the east.

Les Bories is 11 km northwest on the D705 just after the village of Antonne et Trigonant overlooking the river Isle. Guarded by two circular pepperpot towers at the end of an

avenue of trees, this is a classic Renaissance château built in
1497 for Jeanne de Hautefort. Inside are vaulted rooms and
kitchen, and a splendid staircase. Outside are moats, with
terraces overlooking the river, tel. 53-06-00-01. Open 1st
July to 30th September. Out of season it opens for groups
only. The **Château Trigonant** and fourteenth-century
Caussade in a circular rotunda are close by.

Keep on the D705 for 33 km northeast to **Excideuil** (pop.
1900). The original stronghold marked the limits of the
southern Périgord and the beginning of the Limousin. It was
built in the eleventh century as a wooden strongpoint by the
viscounts of Limoges. Then they erected one stone keep and
another in the twelfth century with a strong wall linking the
two. Richard Coeur de Lion tried to take the fortress in 1182
but failed. Philippe le Bel owned it in 1303, and for the next
century it changed hands many times. In 1356 the English
army succeeded in taking it only for Du Guesclin later to evict
them. Local seigneurs in the Middle Ages included the
Gascon Albrets, in 1582 François de Cars (who bought it from
Henri III) and then the Talleyrand-Périgord family. The
château was damaged by fire in 1973 but has been repaired
since. It is a complex building, a blend of rugged military
splendour guarding the vital road to Limoges and the river
Loue, and inside Renaissance splendours. The local
troubadour Giraut de Borneil would have approved! tel.
53-62-95-56. The small town is of interest too. (See tours
from Périgueux.)

As the crow flies **Hautefort** is 15 km away east via the D76
and south on the D704. My wife and I must have viewed this
marvellous huge, majestic château 50 times. For two decades
it has been slowly repaired since it suffered severely from a
fire in 1968. Now there are 50,000 visitors a year to see it
standing in French-style formal gardens in a park of 40
hectares (100 acres) with 15 km of paths and alleys surrounding it. Originally built in the tenth century it still has a twelfth-
century drawbridge, and the main shell dates from 1640.
Inside is a 'court of honour', eighteenth-century tapestries, a
round chapel with 'trompe l'oeil' decorations, a great terrace
and dormer windows, tel. 53-50-51-23. Closed mid-
December to mid-January. From Toussaint (1st November) to

Easter it is open on holidays and Sundays in the afternoon, otherwise from Easter to end October open every day. Six km southeast on the D62 is the ninth-century classified château of Badefols d'Ans, burned by the Nazis in 1944 but since restored.

South of Hautefort, 15 km on the D704 and then west on the N89 towards Périgueux is the château of **Rastignac**, close to the village of La Bachellerie (pop. 720). The minor seigneurs were called *'les bas-chevaliers'*, hence the name of the village. Originally built in 1812-17 it is almost the twin to the presidential White House in Washington. It was badly damaged by fire by the Wehrmacht in 1944 but has since been repaired.

A few km to the east is the seventeent-century **Château de Mellet**, near Beauregard de Terrasson (pop. 500), tel. 53-51-24-94, open 1st July — 31st August. Eight km west of Rastignac is the battlemented **Château of Ajat** plus two romanesque churches.

On the way back on the D89, three km outside Périgueux, is the listed château of **Lieu-Dieu** before you reach the village of Boulazac. Mainly fourteenth/sixteenth century, it has four large circular towers and the main building is on three levels. There is a pigeonnier, ramparts and a moat filled with water.

Château-l'Evêque (pop. 1250) 11 km north on the D939 has a château, now a hotel, which has been the residence of the bishops of Périgueux since it was built in the fourteenth century.

To the southwest along the valley of the river l'Isle is the **Château of Puyferrat** overlooking St Astier (pop. 400). Built in the fifteenth century it is a large rectangular building with two huge round towers. The town and twelfth century church are of note.

Neuvic (pop. 3000) 10 km southeast has a sixteenth-century château, now a medical research centre, but open for viewing only on 11th July and 7th August in the afternoons, tel. 53-81-21-11.

Bergerac

To the far west of Bergerac is Montaigne country, where the great philospher and his family lived in the sixteenth-century.

It is well worth a visit towards St Emilion to see his countryside, *'Mon métier et mon art, c'est vivre'* ('To know how to live is all my calling and all my art.') North of Montcaret is the little village of **Saint Michel de Montaigne** (pop. 300) where the rebuilt château, badly damaged by fire in 1884, stands on the north side. His sixteenth-century library in a circular tower above the chapel should be visited tel. 53-58-63-93. His heart is buried in the twelfth-century Romanesque church in the village, Closed on Tuesday and most of January/February.

Due north of Bergerac, reached by the D709 and then signed for Issac (pop. 400) is the **Château de Montréal**, which in the ninth century (then called Château-Noir) was sacked by the Normans. The river, La Crempse, flows eastwards from Mussidan for many miles, and the valley road once linked Bergerac with Mussidan. The English troops garrisoned Montréal on several occasions during the Hundred Years War. Destroyed in the fourteenth century, rebuilt by François de Pontbriand in the sixteenth century, taken by the Catholics in the religious wars, the château has survived. The early fortifications and double ramparts of the eleventh/twelfth century, the Renaissance lodgings, tall round tower and sixteenth-century Chapelle de la Sainte-Epine are well worth a visit. Claude de Pontbriant, Seigneur de Montréal, accompanied Jacques Cartier on their second expedition to Canada, and named and founded the city of Montreal. Tel. 53-81-11-03 the château is open 1st July to 30th September and for groups out of season by arrangement.

To the northeast of Bergerac, east of the main N21, lie two classic châteaux; **Montastruc** at Lamonzie-Montastruc (pop. 400), built in the thirteenth century, dismantled during the Hundred Years War, rebuilt in 1475; and 10 km north, **La Gaubertie**, mainly sixteenth- and seventeenth-century, nearby St Martin des Combes (pop. 150). They are both close to the D21 overlooking the river Caudau.

To the east of Bergerac, and north of Lalinde (pop. 3000) is the fourteenth-century **Château de Baneuil**, with a ruined Roman keep (and noted eleventh-century church), tel. 53-61-08-31, open in August in the afternoon.

Five km south on the other side of the river is the **Château**

153

de Bournazel in the village of Lanquais (pop. 550). The main château buildings are fourteenth- and sixteenth-century with a huge fortified tower, a *'salle d'armes'* (armoury), well furnished apartments, ornate chimneys and dungeons. In the summer this medieval-Renaissance castle-château is floodlit. Tel, 45-25-02-04, closed on Thursdays, open 1st April — 31st October.

Seven km southeast on the D660 guarding the river Coue is the thirteenth- to fifteenth-century Château de Bannes, captured by the English in 1409. With its large round towers, pepperpot turrets, drawbridge and moat it is very photogenic, but unfortunately not open to the public.

Perhaps the most interesting château of the region lies 10 km south of Bergerac. The **Château de Montbazillac**, near the village of the same name (pop. 800) lies on the D13 between the N21 and the D935. Built in 1550 by the Viscount of Riberac, it has been superbly restored by its present owners, the Union de Co-operatives Vinicole de la Dordogne. Set in a large park with a restaurant, wine tasting facilities, a museum (of Protestantism, furniture and of wine) it has all the classic features; battlements, moat, dungeons, crenellated roofs, towers and turrets, *'escalier d'honneur'*, and is very photogenic! Tel. 53-57-06-38, open throughout the year. You cannot come away empty handed so buy a bottle or two of rich golden wine!

Six km southwest of Ribagnac (pop. 200) is the listed fifteenth-century château of **Bridoire**, with ramparts, moat, round towers and grey walls. During the wars of religion Monluc and his Catholic army laid it to waste but the restoration in the nineteenth century has made it a classic again.

Sarlat and the South East

The final castle *'étape'* is based on **Sarlat-la-Canéda** (pop. 10,000). There are a hundred castles or château within a 30 km radius. It has been a difficult task to whittle the selection down to a dozen.

A large triangle to the west of Sarlat is formed by the Dordogne river, the Vézère river running NW/SE and the main road, the D704, from Montignac running north and south. Each side of the triangle is about 30 km. The richest for grottos, abris and cave-paintings is of course the Vézère valley which is covered elsewhere.

The D706 starts opposite Le Bugue (pop. 2800) and gently meanders partly on the east, partly on the west side of the river. The twelfth- to sixteenth-century **Château de Tayac** faces Les Eyzies, and 10 km due east, guarding two tributaries, are the châteaux of **Laussel** (fifteenth- to sixteenth century), **Commarque** (thirteenth-century and mainly ruined by the English troops), and **Puymartin** (mainly fifteenth-century, with ramparts, towers, Flemish tapestries and seventeenth century wall paintings, tel. 53-59-29-97, open 1st April to 30th September). **Marquay** (pop. 400) is a *'village perché'* with superb grottos and Romanesque church with panoramic views of the châteaux. As the crow flies they are only 15 km northwest from Sarlat.

Continuing up the Vézère valley where there are grottos and troglodyte forts and shelters, we come to **Saint Léon sur Vézère** (pop. 350) with two châteaux close by: Clérans, mainly sixteenth-century, and Chabans, sixteenth- to seventeenth-century. This village is well worth a stop not only for the châteaux but also for the Romanesque church, fortified clocktower and thirteenth- and fourteenth-century cemetery (C.V.) See also the Château de Belcayre of the fifteenth and sixteenth century.

The next village is Thonac (pop. 250) which has the superb sixteenth-century Château de Losse opposite on a thirteenth-century château site; moated and towered, it has good tapestries and furnishings. Tel. 53-50-70-38, open 1st July to 18th September.

Montignac (pop. 3100) is 6 km northeast opposite the fabulous Grotte de Lascaux. Just east of Lascaux, near the D704, is the fifteenth-century Château de la Grande-Filolie, with towers, pavilion, chimney-pieces, seventeenth-century furnishings and chapel. On the way south back to Sarlat east of the D704 are a cluster of four good châteaux.

Salignac-Eyvignes (pop. 900) is on the D60 21 km northeast of Sarlat. The château was built before the twelfth century and has been an important fortress guarding the main road between Brive and Sarlat. The keep, ramparts and towers date from the twelfth century. There are vaulted dungeons,

155

terraces, thirteenth-century chapel and great hall with a huge fifteenth-century fireplace, tel. 53-28-81-70. Open 1st April to 15th September, closed on Tuesdays. Well worth a visit; the village has many thirteenth-century houses, convent, and remains of the Abbey of Sainte-Croix.

Four km west is **St Crepin** (pop. 320) with the sixteenth-century Château de Lacipière, and 4 km south, outside the village of Eyvignes, is the Château du Claud, mainly sixteenth-century with a superb sculpted chimney piece, towers and fifteenth-century chapel.

In the hinterland east of Sarlat there are many relatively minor châteaux, at Proissans, Temniac, Carlux and Barbay-roux, but the half dozen south of Sarlat should be on every visitor's itinerary.

Along the river Dordogne starting in the west at **La Buisson** there are châteaux on most promontories. In the Hundred Years War the French might have glared at the English across 250 metres of fastflowing river.

On the north bank are Fages, sixteenth/seventeenth century, and La Roque near St Cyprien. Follow the D703 to **Beynac et Cazenac** which was built in 1140 and was occupied by Richard Coeur de Lion in 1195 and dismantled by Simon de Montfort in 1214. It was reconstructed in the thirteenth-century, restored in the sixteenth and seventeenth century and is one of the military splendours of the Dordogne. It still has a double rampart, moat and barbican. Inside is a superb thirteenth-century vaulted great hall, Romanesque chapel and fifteenth-century wall murals, tel. 53-29-50-40, open from 1st March to 15th November. You can see four other châteaux from the battlements of Beynac — one of the best castle visits in the Périgord!

Just round the river bend is the **Château of Marqueyssac** near the Vezac (pop. 450). The gardens and terrace of the château command superb views along the river. Around the next bend is the beautiful village of **La Roque-Gageac** (pop. 400) with the fifteenth/sixteenth-century Château de Tarde and nineteenth-century Château de la Malartrie (in sixteenth century style). Next is Vitrac (pop. 650) and then the Château de Montfort on a lofty spur overlooking the hamlet of Turnac. Most of the château is fourteenth/fifteenth century but it was much restored in the nineteenth century, a mixture of medieval and Renaissance. During the Hundred Years War it was captured, and recaptured with alternate ownership. Very photogenic but not open to the public.

Now on the final stretch are the previously English-owned châteaux on the south bank of the Dordogne. From west to east starting at **La Buisson** on the D25 is Berbiguières with twelfth-century keep, drawbridge, and circular ramparts (now on the D50) to Les Milandes, fifteenth/sixteenth-century, tel. 53-29-50-73, open from 27th March to 15th October, made famous as Josephine Baker's orphan home. Very close is Castelnaud, mainly twelfth-century, with fourteenth-century keep and huge fifteenth-century tower, recently restored, tel. 53-28-47-69, open 1st May to 15th November. See there the museum of 'La Guerre au Moyen-Age'.

Just on the east side of the Cénac bridge over the river Dordogne is **Domme** (pop. 900) where Simon de Montfort destroyed the château in 1214. It is one of the most interesting **bastide** villages in the Dordogne and is an essential visit. Further east along the D50 are the villages of Groléjac (pop. 500) and Veyrignac (pop. 250) with a listed château of the fourteenth-century with musuem. Partly burned out in 1944 by the Germans, it has been well restored, tel. 53-28-13-56, open all the year except January and February.

Finally 4 km to the east is the **Château of Fénelon** near the village of Sainte-Mondane (pop. 250). Built mainly in the thirteenth century and repaired in the sixteenth/seventeenth century, the two large towers, fortified gateways and double ramparts make Fénelon one of the Dordogne's showpieces. There is a library, chapel, large outside staircases, and terraces with balustrades. The views along the river are superb. There is also a museum of vintage cars, tel. 53-29-84-04, open all the year.

If you are staying at Sarlat or Domme or Belvès then at some stage you will be visiting the attractive bastide town of **Monpazier** in the south of the Dordogne. A few km south are two listed châteaux, that of St Germain overloking the river Dropt, and the mighty Château de Biron. My wife and I have visited it a dozen times and would be happy to look over it annually! The Gontaut family were one of the four powerful

157

families of the twelfth century and built this enormous château on the village hill. The Albigensians took it in 1211, Simon de Montfort in 1217 and the English owned it during the fourteenth and fifteenth centuries. The keep is probably Roman, making it the oldest castle in the Dordogne. Lots to see, marvellous views, tel. 53-53-44-35, open all the year except Tuesdays.

The Lot valley east of the Dordogne has several châteaux of note. **Castelnau** claims to be the number two fortress of France — a huge redbrick castle dominating the rivers Dordogne and Bave. It is well worth a visit combined with the smaller château of Montal near St Céré.

East of Souillac along the Dordogne valley are La Treyne, Lacave, and Creysse along the enchanting river road to Carennac.

Châteaux at a glance

The most powerful	Beynac
The most interesting, historically	Biron
The most elegant	Jumilhac-le-Grand
The grandest	Hautefort
The largest	Castelnau (Lot)

If any readers have differing views my publisher and I will be delighted to hear from them. Many of the 1200 castles are not only privately owned but also discreetly hidden in parkland and woods. You can expect to pay 20 francs per adult for a guided tour of about one hour.

The grandest churches in the Dordogne

With eight hundred churches, many of them in the Romanesque style of the tenth to twelfth century, it is difficult to decide which should be included in this chapter. The French authorities have helped with their classifications of MH i.e. *Monument Historique*, and IMH i.e. logged in the *Inventory of Monuments Historiques*. I have shown them in a northern, central and southern section with brief descriptive notes. The Cistercian abbeys in particular in my view should be seen, above all the one at **Cadouin**. Among the unique curiosities in the Dordogne are the three intriguing *'Lanternes des Morts'* to be seen in Sarlat, Cherveix-Cubas and Atur. Nobody is absolutely sure what they were built for — since it was/is difficult to get coffins in and out!

If I had time for only one visit, then I would choose without a doubt **Rocamadour** (southeast of Souillac). It is a cluster of religious buildings with seven churches and chapels clinging to the steep cliff face, steeped in legend and history, and is still the second pilgrimage site in France.

The finest fortified church, which we recently visited, is the twelfth-century abbey dominating the small village of St Amand-de-Coly a few km east of Montignac. Minor repairs continue all the time but it is well worth a visit on the way to Lascaux. The classic simplicity of the twelfth-century Benedictine priory at St Léon sur Vézère should be seen. It is on the river-grotto route of the D706 between Montignac and Les Eyzies.

Many Périgourdin churches have massive bell-towers (beffroi), for instance at Brantôme Abbey, Issigeac, Thiviers, St Avit-Senieur, Chancelade Abbey, Les Eyzies-de-Tayac and Prats-de-Périgord. Look at the way the architects of the bastide towns, who were not allowed to build a château for defence, were able to make their church in the central square a veritable stronghold. **Beaumont-du-Périgord** and **Monpazier** are classic examples. Imagine the frightened peasantry from the neighbouring undefended hamlets taking sanctuary in the bastide town churches. Agonac (north of Périgueux) church of St Martin has many defensive features, as do Allas-lès-Mines, and Carsac-de-Gurson. Some of the major churches, such as **Chancelade Abbey**, have a *'son-et-lumière'* pageant in mid-summer.

Look for the churches with roofs made of stone *'lauzes'* — heavy rectangular tiles made of the local stone, needing very strong supporting wooden beams. They include Ajat south of Périgueux, Groléjac, Carsac-Aillac and Beynac's fifteenth-century chapel.

Many churches were (or are) pilgrim sites. **Rocamadour** is the most famous, then Cadouin, Azerat, Auriac-du-Périgord (St Rémy) – see Chapter Fifteen. Churches with cloisters include Cadouin, St Front (Périgueux), Boschaud Abbey, Carennac (Lot), St Jean de Côle (alas private) and Bergerac (wine museum). Churches with curious animal carvings are Sadillac (south of Bergerac) and the Priory of St Julien near Cenac.

One of the best Romanesque church tours in the Dordogne is in the valley of the Vézère. **Les Eyzies-de-Tayac** church is twelfth-century, built of ochre-coloured stone with two crenellated defensive towers. North on the D706 to Plazac, a medieval village where the bishops of Périgueux built a stronghold to protect the church; see too the presbytery and sixteenth-century frescoes. Then to St Léon sur Vézère where the church dates from St Bernard's time (1090-1153), of a grand simplicity, again of ochre stone. Next to St Amand de Coly where the huge fortified abbey is of the twelfth century, and finally to Fanlac which has lauze-roofed houses, pigeonniers and a twelfth century fortified church with a clock tower. The five churches and villages can be visited in half a day. You can get a leaflet with details from the local tourist office at Montignac and Les Eyzies.

The northern sector

Bussière-Badil (north of Nontron) eleventh-century Romanesque, octagonal belltower, buttresses.

Champniers et Reilhac (north of Nontron).

Cherval (southwest of Nontron) twelfth-century, four-domed church.

La Gonterie-Boulonneix (south of Nontron) church and priory of Belaygue.

Grand Brassac (southwest of Nontron) thirteenth-century fortified church.

Javerlhac (northwest of Nontron) abbey-church of St Robert.

Lempzours (southeast of Nontron) with two out of three original domes.

Ligueux (southeast of Nontron) 1185 convent for Benedictine nuns.

Mareuil (northwest of Brantôme) thirteenth-century Romanesque.

Paussac (southwest of Nontron) Romanesque church.

St Martial Viveyrol (northwest of Nontron) powerful fortified twelfth-century church.

St Jean de Côle (south of Nontron) eleventh-century priory and bell tower.

Excideuil (south east of Thiviers) Benedictine priory of St Thomas.

The central sector around Périgueux

Agonac (north) St Martin's church, bell tower.

Ajat (east) stone lauzed roof, romanesque church.

Atur (south) twelfth-century church and Lantern of the Dead.

Auriac du Périgord (east) fifteenth-century Romanesque.

Badefols d'Ans (east) domed twelfth-century church.

Brantôme Abbey and Museum of Sacred Art (north) founded by Charlemagne.

Chancelade Abbey (north) twelfth-century Augustinian priory.

La Chapelle-Gonaquet and Merlande Priory (north west).

Cherveix-Cubas (east) twelfth-century St Martial-Laborie and Lantern of the Dead.

Lisle (northwest) sixteenth-century Gothic vault.

Périgueux Cathedral St Front, cloister, five superb domes, 12 pepperpot towers, and St Etienne de la Cité.

Riberac (west) two churches of note.

St Astier (southwest) see bell tower.

St Privat (west of Riberac) twelfth-century Benedictine priory.

Toutoirac (east) twelfth century Benedictine abbey.

Southern sector around Bergerac and Sarlat

Baneuil (East of Bergerac) domed twelfth-century church.

Beaumont (southeast of Bergerac) St Front church built 1272 by the English.

Belves (southwest of Sarlat) thirteenth-century Benedictine Priory.

Cadouin Abbey (between Sarlat and Bergerac), twelfth-century cloisters, pilgrimage museum.

Groléjac-Cénac (south of Sarlat) troglodyte church of Caudon.

161

St Amand-de-Coly (north of Sarlat) yellow limestone, fortified twelfth century church.

St Leon-sur-Vézère (northwest of Sarlat) yellow limestone, fortified twelfth-century priory, belltower, frescoes.

Limeuil (between Sarlat and Bergerac) domed church of St Martin from 1194.

Sarlat twelfth-century St Sacerdos Cathedral, also Lanterne des Morts tower.

Bergerac twelfth-century cloisters of Recollects, now wine council building.

Tayac (west of Sarlat) twelfth-century fortified church of Les Eyzies.

Paunat (near Tremolat on river Dordogne) twelfth-century of St Martial.

St Geniès (north of Sarlat) fourteenth-century frescoes in Cheyland chapel.

St Avit-Senieur (southwest of Cadouin) fourteenth century fortified chruch.

St Cyprien (west of Sarlat) large twelfth-century Augustinian church.

Carsac-Aillac (southeast of Sarlat), restored with stone 'lauze' roofs.

St. Julien-de-Lampon (southeast of Sarlat) sixteenth century frescoes in church.

The Lot – eastern valley of Dordogne

Souillac St. Mary's Abbey of twelfth-century, superb doorway carvings.

Rocamadour complex of seven chapels, churches with frescoes, black virgin, etc.

Carennac cloisters of twelfth-century church of St Pierre.

St Céré church of Ste-Sperie rebuilt in gothic style of seventeenth-century.

Gourdon Franciscan church of fourteenth-century.

Part Four:
Culture and Language

CHAPTER FIFTEEN:
FESTIVALS, FAIRS AND EVENTS

There's more to Dordogne than castles, churches, green valleys and rivers. There are museums, folklore activities, summer concerts and theatre. You can watch the local artisans at work using centuries-old techniques and there are even several pilgrimages held every year.

There are no less than 30 museums scattered across the department and I have placed them geographically rather than by subject. For the smaller villages and towns I have included, in brackets, other sights to make a more rounded visit for all the family. In late summer, early September, every village has its *fête*, though these vary enormously in noise, colour and interest.

You would expect the major towns of Périgueux and Bergerac to have a season of cultural events — and they do! Between July and September there are always 50 shows and events. The theatre in Périgueux is at the Palais des Fêtes in the Avenue d'Aquitaine, tel. 53-53-18-17, and their music society 'Amis de la Musique' is at 21, Rue P. Sémard, tel. 53-08-30-51. Concerts, plays, talks, and art exhibitions are held throughout the year. Bergerac has thirty different cultural associations and societies and each year there is an Art Festival from July – September in the old *'moulin des cordeliers'*.

Throughout the Dordogne there are music and art festivals and celebrations of local folklore activities which will be of interest to the visitor. Some I have tracked down are in small villages, which can be more attractive. They are shown roughly north to south.

Bussières-Badil (pop. 600) 15 km north of Nontron has a *'Fête folklorique des battages d'antan'* (Threshing festival).

163

Piegut-Pluviers (pop. 1500) 10 km north of Nontron has a folklore group active in summer with dances and accordion contests.

Abjat-sur-Bandiat (pop. 700) 10 km northeast of Nontron has a theatre and dance season in summer.

Nontron (pop. 4000) has a theatre, a folklore festival in July and many other jolly activities, fairs and *fêtes*.

St Jean de Côle (pop. 300) southeast of Nontron has concerts throughout August.

Excideuil (pop. 1900) 40 km southeast of Nontron has an active summer programme of concerts, *fêtes* and cultural activities.

Sainte Croix-le-Mareuil (pop. 150) 15 km southwest of Nontron has a folklore *fête* on 19th August.

Chancelade (pop. 2400) just northwest of Périgueux has a festival of music in June and religious musical concerts in the handsome twelfth-century abbey church throughout the season.

Mayac (pop. 270) 20 km northeast of Périgueux has an active folklore group.

Peyrignac (pop. 350) 35 km east of Périgueux has a theatrical *'troupe'* called *'Tout Peyrignac sur les planches'*.

La Bachellerie (pop. 720) close to the above, has a theatre with a full season of *fêtes*, exhibitions and fairs.

Breuilh (pop. 120) has a folklore festival at Christmas.

Sainte Alvère (pop. 750) 35 km southeast of Périgueux has summer open air theatre and church concerts. In December they hold their *fête 'du Peyrol'*.

Riberac (pop. 4000) 30 km west of Périgueux has a major fair-exhibition alternate years in August. In July concerts of medieval music are held and fêtes etc called *'Nuits d'août à Riberac'*.

La Roche Chalais (pop. 3000) is just southwest of Riberac and has an active folklore programme *'histoire et traditions populaires'*.

Montpon-Ménéstrol (pop. 6000) is 20 km south of the above. Organ recitals are held in the Romanesque church of Ménéstrol during the season.

South of Bergerac are three more villages with cultural activities:

Faux (pop. 600) has a folklore and theatrical group.

Lanquais (pop. 550) has a theatre and full programme in *'La Grange'*.

Pomport (pop. 670) has a summer programme of folklore dances.

Moving eastwards to Sarlat, this progressive town has an antiques exhibition (20th Aug – 20th Sept), a national photographic art exhibition each year in July-August, a theatre festival throughout August and in midsummer, concerts and art and artisanal exhibitions. Meyrals (pop. 400) 10 km west of Sarlat has summer concerts in La Rougerie manor-house. St Amand de Coly (pop. 300) 25 km north of Sarlat has summer concerts in the fortified abbey-church. The *'Association des amis de St Amand'* produces cultural events, art exhibitions and artisanal displays.

Villamblard just east of Mussidan offers courses in wood or stone sculpture at 'Chabinel', Beleymas, 24140 Villamblard, tel. 53-81-97-58. A 30-hour limited course over a week currently costs 1000 francs.

Two leading Folklore Societies near Périgueux are 'Les Croquants d'Escornabiou', Sarazy-Coulouniex, tel. 53-08-42-71, and 'Lou Chabridous', 43 Rue des Pinsons, Notre Dame de Sanilhac, tel. 53-09-08-20. The Périgord is rich in romantic historic legends, songs and dances going back to Troubadour days.

Museums northern region

Nontron (pop. 4000). In the château is the intriguing Doll Museum (*'jeux d'antan'*, the toys and games over the centuries) founded by Marie-Camille de Monneron, tel. 53-56-20-80. Closed Tuesdays.

Mareuil (pop. 1200) 20 km southwest of Nontron has a

museum in the château of Mareuil devoted to souvenirs of Marshal Lannes (Duke of Montebello), one of Napoleon's favourites. (This castle, that of Beauregard, and the twelfth--century church of St Pardoux, make the town worth a detour.)

Hautefort (pop. 800). Midsummer exhibition of textile weaving in church.

Bourdeilles (pop. 650) just southwest of Brantôme has an excellent sixteenth-century collection of furniture, tapestries, armoury and paintings at the great château, tel. 53-53-44-35. Closed Tuesdays. (Superb panoramic views from terraces, picturesque village.)

Brantôme (pop. 2000) has the Musée Desmoulin, tel. 53-05-70-21, open 1st April to end September. Closed on Tuesdays. Mainly local prehistory, but also paintings, ceramics and engravings. (See fifteenth-century abbey, many medieval buildings, twelfth-century Romanesque church, many pretty rivers which thread through the town, plus gastronomic delights.)

Périgueux (pop. 40,000) has two museums; Musée du Périgord in the Cours Tourny, tel. 53-52-16-42. Closed Tuesdays, one of the major prehistory museums in France, look for Chancelade Man; and the Museum of Military History, tel. 53-53-47-36, 28 Rue des Farges, closed Sundays.

St Jean de Côle (pop. 300) 20 km southeast of Nontron has a small museum of daily life, traditions and folklore of bygone ages. (One of the best villages in the Dordogne — listed château, abbey, cloisters, artisans, horse races etc.)

Thiviers (pop. 4200) 25 km southeast of Nontron has a museum of foie gras called 'Maison de l'Oie et du Canard', tel. 53-55-12-50. Open Whitsun to 30th Sept. Closed Sundays and Mondays. (See twelfth-century church and fortified presbytery and Château de Vaucocour).

Teyjat (pop. 400) 8 km northwest of Nontron has a small prehistory museum. (Listed Grotto of La Mairie.)

La Tour Blanche (pop. 450) 25 km of Nontron has the

Musée des Records, tel. 53-91-11-98, open July-August. (Listed 'donjon' – keep and fourteenth-century Château of Jovelle.)

Varaignes (pop. 440) northwest of Nontron has the Musée des Arts et Traditions Populaires et du Tissage (weaving), tel. 53-56-35-76. Closed Tuesdays, located in the thirteenth-century château. (Great place for *fêtes*, artisans and turkeys!)

Museums central region

Auriac-du-Périgord (pop. 320) a hamlet 30 km east of Périgueux has the Eco-musée de l'Abeille (bees and beekeeping), tel. 53-51-86-34. Open 1st June to 30th Sept. (Château de la Faye, fortified twelfth-century church, pilgrimage.)

Chancelade (pop. 2400) 10 km northwest of Périgueux. Important museum of sacred art in the twelfth-century abbey. (Festival of music in June.)

Douzillac (pop. 700) is 20 km southwest of Périgueux. It has a small museum devoted to the traditions of the French Foreign Legion. (See Château de Mauriac and visit the onion fair.)

La Cassagne (pop. 100) a hamlet 25 km northeast of Sarlat, has a small museum at La Grange Dimière (where the old tithes were collected) devoted to the works of M. Sem, a caricature artist, tel. 53-51-66-43, open 14th July-1st Sept. in the afternoons. (Pleasant *plan d'eau*, canoeing, and camping site.)

Montignac (pop. 3100) 30 km southeast of Périgueux on the river Vézère, the Museum Eugène Le Roy, tel. 53-51-82-60 is closed in January and on Sundays. In Rue Septembre, it has a collection of souvenirs of the famous novelist who wrote 'Jacquou le Croquant' and other works. The museum of Périgourdin Folklore, and Musée de Regourdou and Lascaux II are nearby.

Mussidan (pop. 3250) 30 km southwest of Périgueux has the Museum of Arts and Popular Traditions, a collection by Dr A. Voulgre, tel. 53-81-23-55. Closed Tuesdays. At the town hall

167

is a small collection of paintings of the brothers Beaupuy de la Bacharetie.

Saint Privat-des-Près (pop. 700) is 10 km southwest of Riberac and has a real village museum with tools and implements showing *'la vie du village'*, tel. 53-91-22-87. Open June – September in the afternoons. (A superb fortified twelfth-century church.)

Sorges (pop. 900) 20 km northeast of Périgueux has the Eco-museum of the Truffle, tel. 53-05-90-11. Open all the year, closed Tuesdays.

Villefranche-de-Lonchat (pop. 750) 30 km west of Bergerac. Local history and folklore museum, tel. 53-80-77-25, at the Mairie, open July – Sept. but closed weekends. (Old English *bastide* with gothic listed church.)

Villamblard (pop. 850) is halfway between Périgueux and Bergerac.

Montagnac la Crempse (pop. 400) is a hamlet 8 km south with a little village museum, Hameau de la Grane, tel. 53-81-93-19 to arrange visits.

Museums southern region

Bergerac has three quite different museums; Musée d'Interêt National du Tabac, tel. 53-63-04-13, closed on Mondays, otherwise open all the year round. The region round Bergerac produces much of the *'tabac'* that goes into *'Disque Bleu'* and *'Gitanes'* cigarettes. The museum is situated in the seventeenth-century convent des Dames de la Foi. The Maison du Vin is in the *Cloître* (cloisters *des Recollets*), tel. 53-57-12-57. Open July and August, out of season by appointment. Try to taste the wide variety of local wines. The Museum of Sacred Art is next door to the church of St Jacques. Open all the year at usual 'church' times.

Fénelon and Sainte Mondane. Museum about Archbishop Fénelon of Cambrai (b. 1651) and vintage motorcars.

Belvès (pop. 1600) equidistant from Bergerac and Sarlat, south of the river. In the *'maison des Consuls'* is a small museum of local history. (The pretty town is on a hill with ramparts, belfry, keeps and listed churches.)

Beynac-et-Cazenac (pop. 400). Museum of Prehistory. Open 15th June – 15th Sept. (Superb thirteenth-century château overlooking the river Dordogne.)

Le Buisson-de-Cadouin (pop. 2000). Museum of Sacred Art in twelfth-century abbey in Cadouin south of river Dordogne.

Couze-et-Saint-Front (pop. 1000) on river Dordogne has a museum of the History of Paper-making situated in an old paper windmill, Moulin de la Roque. (See troglodyte village.)

Domme (pop. 900) south of Sarlat has the Musée Paul Reclus, of Art and Popular Traditions, tel. 53-28-30-18. Open Open 1st April – 31st October. In the Porte des Tours is the Prison des Templiers (visits at 5 pm), tel. 53-28-37-09. 1st April – 30th Sept. (Domme is one of the most interesting *bastide* towns in the Dordogne, perched on a rocky hill dominating the river Dordogne.)

Eymet (pop. 3000) 30 km southwest of Bergerac has a museum of prehistory, local folklore and traditions, armoury and coins situated in the château, tel. 53-23-93-33. Open all year except Sunday mornings. (*Bastide* town, Bergerac wines, local artisans.)

Doissat (pop. 150) a hamlet near Belvès has a museum of nuts in the château. Logical since this region grows more nuts than anywhere else in Europe.

Les Eyzies de Tayac-Sireuil (pop. 900) on the river Vézère, west of Sarlat, has three museums. Prehistory in Château de Tayac, tel. 53-06-97-03, open all year except Tuesdays. Musée de Spéléologie (pot-holing), tel. 53-29-68-42, open July-August except Saturdays. The museum at Laugerie Bas of *stratigraphie* (archeology). Also the Garden of Medicinal Plants (biology), tel. 53-06-97-24, open 10th March-23rd October. Children will appreciate the Parc Naturel in the valley of the Gorge d'Enfer where they can talk to the modern animal versions of the prehistoric drawings, including bison, hemiones, and Prejaski horses!

Montcaret (pop. 1000) is 30 km west of Bergerac. The Gallo-Roman museum has splendid Roman mosaics, sculptures, hypocauste, and thermal baths, tel. 53-08-00-94, open all the year, but closed Tuesdays out of season. (Visit the Cave-co-operative, see the eleventh-century Romanesque church and local artisans.)

Monbazillac (pop. 800) is 12 km south of Bergerac. The sixteenth-century château houses not only the wine co-operative, but also the Museum of Protestantism, wine, prehistory, furniture, caricatures by M. Sem and a local map collection. Well worth a visit, taste the wines and lunch at the restaurant in the château afterwards, tel. 53-57-06-38. Open all the year.

St Avit-Senieur (pop. 400) is equidistant from Sarlat and Bergerac, south of the river Dordogne. The Geological Museum is open July – August, tel. 53-33-32-27, closed on Mondays. (A 'perched' village with eleventh-century abbey church and Bergerac wines.)

Peyzac-le-Moustier (pop. 120) on the Vézère just north of Les Eyzies has a small prehistory museum, tel. 53-04-86-21, open July – August.

Sarlat-la-Canéda (pop. 10,000) has the Museum of Sacred Art at the Chapel des Pénitents Blancs. Closed Sunday mornings, open from Easter to 30th Sept. An oddity is the Musée Aquarium, tel. 53-59-44-58, open all the year.

Sergeac (pop. 150) 15 km northwest of Sarlat has a small museum at Castelmerle of prehistory and paleonthology. (Half a dozen listed grottos and twelfth-century church.)

Tamnies (pop. 300) near Sergeac has a local history and prehistoric museum at the Mairie. (This is *foie gras* country. Visit local producers.)

Thonac (pop. 250) near Sergeac has the Prehistoric Art Museum of Thot, tel. 53-53-44-35, open all the year except Mondays out of season.

Tursac (pop. 240) north of Les Eyzies. The original museum of art has been moved to Sarlat. The Prehisto-Park, tel. 53-50-73-19 is closed Dec-Feb, open rest of year.

Villefranche-du Périgord (pop. 800). This delightful *bastide* town on the southern border is well known for its mushrooms and *cèpes*. Appropriate then is the Maison du Chataignier, Marrons et Champignons devoted to history and varieties, tel. 53-29-98-37, closed on Mondays, Sundays p.m.

Handcrafts

The rural population of the Dordogne has always excelled at regional craft work and there follows a summary of where the visitor should look for attractive and unusual 'objets d'art' in the countryside. Several centres or ateliers provide 'stages' or work-classes for interested visitors, using traditional methods and materials.

St Jean-de-Côle – pottery classes in this superbly pretty village southeast of Nontron. Ask for *'Association les amis du Vieux St Jean'*.

Villars – pottery ateliers with annual artisan exhibition of work from 8th July to 15th August each year.

Couze – hand-made craft papers. This small town on the river Dordogne has been making paper, called *'papier de Hollande'* from the fifteenth century. In an old paper-mill there is a museum of paper-making over the centuries.

Mussidan – ceramics manufacturing club has 'stages' for visitors. The town is 30 km northwest of Bergerac.

Périgueux – visit the Créateurs et Artisans d'Art du Périgord at 4 Rue St Front.

St Amand-de-Coly – 30 km north of Sarlat. Ask for the *'Association des amis de St Amand'* who hold frequent exhibitions of handcrafts and paintings/engravings/sculptures.

Montignac – on the river Vézère. Besides its prehistoric reputation it has a tradition of *'artisanat'* skills, many can be seen in the museum *'folklorique périgourdin'*.

Sorges – northeast of Périgueux has a major summer exhibition of art and wide variety of Périgordan artisan skills.

Plazac – northwest of Sarlat, near Montignac, has silkscreen printing classes with gîtes and camping available.

St Vincent-Jalmontiers – a village 20 km southwest of Riberac in the valley of the river Rizonne. In the *village de vacances* (holiday village) is a permanent art study centre open to artists and students alike above the age of 16. Classes include pottery, weaving, painting on silk, macramé, basket-making and wicker-work, jewellry making, leather-working, wood and metal working. Classes usualy consist of three people only. The price for tuition and work facilities in the various ateliers is 650 francs per week. This includes two hours, intensive tuition, plus constant monitoring of progress and six hours, a day access to the atelier-studios, with two hours supervised work in the atelier-studio. Food and lodging is very economical in a six-person *'gîte rural'* or campsite or *'chambre d'hôte'* (bed and breakfast).

Marnac – a hamlet with seventeenth-century houses called *'La Grande Marque'* on the river Dordogne halfway between Domme and Tremolat. Art classes are held for design, lithography, oil painting, gouache, clay-moulding techniques and sculpture. They are of a high standard with all kinds of government certificates to prove it! A one-week class in the period February to April costs 2100 francs per person inclusive of 40 hours, tuition during the week, complete pension including wine and coffee. An absolute bargain! From June to September inclusive a week's course is upped to 2400 francs per person. You pay for basic material needed for lithography and sculpture. Apply to Bernard Devaux or Nicole Martin who will meet you at the station at Siorac en Périgord.

Soudat – a hamlet 20 km northwest of Nontron where adult painting classes are held with the subject *'Le Paysage'* – the countryside. A week's course is held each year during the four-week period 31st July – 27th August. Courses are for a maximum of seven people, from Monday to Saturday inclusive and cost 2820 francs per person inclusive of demi-pension for that week in a two-star hotel in Nontron – and paper, paints, and brushes are provided.

Other *'artisanat'* villages

Beauroane – 8 km north of Mussidan – pottery.

Besse – just north of Villefranche-du-Périgord – wood working, carving.

Coursac – southwest of Périgueux has a notable bronze foundry and weavers.

Tursac – on the river Vézère has several local sculptors.

Meyrais – west of Sarlat has a carpet-weaver, and wool-spinners.

Lembras – northeast of Bergerac has several potters.

La Coquille – north of Thiviers has skilled iron and metal workers.

Bussière-Badil – north of Nontron has an Easter pottery fair.

Beynac-et-Cazenac – on the river Dordogne southeast of Sarlat has a collection of stone sculptors, glass-blowers and potters.

Chancelade – just northwest of Périgueux has silk-screen printers (*serigraphie*) and silk-weavers.

Boulazac – east of Périgueux, has an artisanat centre with various skills.

Boisse – east of Eymet, near Issigeac has potters and glass-blowers.

La Chapelle-Gonaquel – just north west of Périgueux has various weavers.

La Douze – southeast of Périgueux has wicker and basket workers.

Paussac et Saint Vivien – northwest of Périgueux has some potters.

Razac-sur-l'Isle – southwest of Périgueux has art exhibitions throughout the summer.

Saint-Germain-des-Près – south of Thiviers has wood carvers, doll makers and weavers.

Beauregard-de-Terrasson — northeast of Terrasson le Villedieu combines a fête with exhibitions of several local artisans on 15th August.

Also at Thiviers, many in Sarlat, Riberac, Monpazier, Marquay, Le Buisson-de-Cadouin, Eymet, Montcaret, St Avit-Sénieur, St Cernin-de-l'Herm and Vezac.

In the château of Varaignes, 15 km northwest of Nontron is the Museum of Popular Arts and Traditions — particularly spinning and weaving, tel. 53-56-35-76, closed Tuesdays.

The local market has a weaver and heddler fair at Whitsun. At Saint-Privat-des-Près, southwest of Riberac, is the museum of artisanat tools, implements and scenes of medieval life. Open June – Sept inclusive, tel. 53-91-22-87. In the château of Nontron is the doll museum and *'jeux d'antan'* i.e. the household toys of the past, tel. 53-53-44-35, closed Tuesdays out of season. The museums at Mussidan (A. Voulgré collection) and at Domme have collections of popular traditions and arts.

Saints and pilgrimages

Many rural departments of France, perhaps in places where traditions and spiritual beliefs still remain strong, have places of pilgrimage. To those shrines the faithful wend their way once or more a year to make their pleas or render thanks. I have discovered a dozen such places of pilgrimage with the hope that they may be of interest to travellers to the region. From north to south they are as follows:

Mareuil (pop. 1200) southwest of Nontron has an annual pilgrimage on 8th Sept. at the church of St Pardoux-de-Mareuil, a beautiful twelfth-century church.

Saint-Raphael (pop. 90) a hamlet equidistant southeast of Nontron and northeast from Périgueux (near castles of Hautefort and Excideuil) has a popular pilgrimage to Saint Rémy whose tomb is in the village church.

Saint-Aquiln (pop. 400) 15 km west of Périgueux has the pilgrimage to St-Eutrope at the fortified Gothic church (see dolmen and Château de Puyferrat).

Douchapt (pop. 250) is a few km north west of Saint-Aquila. Annual pilgrimage to the chapel of Notre Dame. The village has the towers of Vernode, a Romanesque church and windmills to look at.

Notre Dame de Sanilhac (pop. 2000) is 10 km south of Périgueux. The annual fête and pilgrimage take place on the Sunday after 8th September at the seventeenth-century church Notre Dame des Vertus. She is called '*la vierge trouvée*'.

On the east side of Périgueux there are three more places of pilgrimage.

Brouchard (pop. 200) has its pilgrimage on the second Sunday in September.

Chatres (pop. 200) has its fête and pilgrimage on 8th September.

Auriac du Périgord (pop. 300) has a pilgrimage in September to Saint Rémy at the twelfth-century Romanesque chapel of the same name, popularised by Eugène Le Roy in his book 'Jacquou le Croquant'.

Moving further south to Laveyssière (pop. 100) northwest of Bergerac, the annual fête and pilgrimage take place on 8th September.

Tursac (pop. 240) the prehistoric village northwest of Sarlat is the scene of the September pilgrimage of Fonpeyrine to the fourteenth-century chapel of that name.

A few km southeast of Sarlat on the river Dordogne is Sainte-Mondane (pop. 250) which has been a major pilgrimage centre from the ninth century. The saint came from Bordeaux and was mother of St Sacerdos, Bishop of Limoges and patron of Sarlat. She was killed by the Saracens but her grotto by the sacred fountain under the rocks is still venerated. Finally Belvès (pop. 1600) 25 km southwest of Sarlat has its annual pilgrimage on 8th September at the modern chapel, Notre Dame-de-Capelou. A sacred fountain is nearby. Rocamadour (Lot) of course has several major pilgrimages during the year.

175

CHAPTER SIXTEEN:
FINDING OUT MORE

All the towns in the Dordogne have a tourist office or a 'syndicat d'initiative'. Some, such as in Périgueux or Sarlat, are highly sophisticated, but many others are primitive. However when open, they are as helpful as they can be. Many of them are closed out of season, and nearly all of them close for lunch from 12 noon to 2 p.m. Some open on Saturdays. I have listed in alphabetical order the towns and villages where they are to be found. (M) stands for Mairie, and (V) for guided visits available.

Périgord noir i.e. the southeast

Belvès	53-29-01-40	(M)
Beynac	53-29-50-75	(M) (V)
Le Bugue	53-07-20-48	
Le Buisson	53-22-06-09	
Domme	53-28-37-09	(V)
Les Eyzies	53-06-97-05	(V)
Montignac	53-51-82-60	(V)
Rouffignac	53-05-46-46	(M)
Ste-Alvère	53-22-71-25	(M)
St-Cyprien	53-30-36-09	(M)
Sarlat	53-59-27-67	(V)
Siorac en Périgord	53-31-60-29	(M)
Terrasson	53-50-37-56	

Périgord vert i.e. the north

La Coquille	53-52-80-56	(M)
Brantôme	53-05-80-52	(V)
Bussière-Badil	53-60-52-07	(M)

Excideuil	53-62-95-56	(M) (V)
Javerlhac	53-56-30-18	(M)
Jumilhac-le-Grand	53-52-55-43	
Lanouaille	53-52-60-21	(M)
Mareuil sur Belle	53-60-91-20	(M) (V)
Nontron	53-56-25-50	(M)
St Jean de Côle	53-62-30-21	(M)
Villars	53-54-82-04	(M)
Thiviers	53-55-12-50	
Varaignes	53-56-31-05	(M)
Bourdeilles	53-03-73-13	(M)
Riberac	53-90-03-10	(V)
St-Aulaye	53-90-81-33	(M)

Périgord blanc i.e. in the centre

Montpon-Ménéstrol	53-80-30-21	(M)
Mussidan	53-81-04-07	(M)
Neuvic	53-81-52-11	
Périgueux	53-53-10-63	(V)
St-Astier	53-54-11-18	(M)
St Léon sur l'Isle	53-80-65-18	(M)
Sorges	53-05-90-11	(Truffle centre visits)
Hautefort	53-50-40-27	

Périgord pourpre i.e. around Bergerac

Beaumont du Périgord	53-22-39-12	(M) (V)
Bergerac	53-57-03-11	(V)
Eymet	53-23-74-95	(M) (V)
Issigeac	53-58-70-32	(M)
Lalinde	53-61-08-55	
Saussignac	53-27-92-27	(M)
Villamblard	53-81-90-18	(M)
Villefranche de Lonchat	53-80-77-25	(M)
Monpazier	53-22-60-38	(M) (V)

Limeuil   53-22-04-66 (M)
Villefranche du   53-29-98-37
    Périgord

The Lot (Dordogne valley)

Bretenoux   65-38-59-53 (M)
Carennac   65-38-58-12 (M)
Gourdon   65-41-06-40 (V)
Padirac-Alvignac   65-38-73-60
Rocamadour   65-33-62-80 (V)
Saint-Céré   65-38-11-85
Souillac   65-37-81-56

Non-cultural events during the year in the Dordogne

Every town and village in the Dordogne has its own gala day and evening during the summer. It may be a *'fête locale'*, a *'fête patronale'*, a *'répas périgourdin'*, a *'fête champêtre'* (a communal evening feast in the open air, often in a park), a *'fête votive'* or a *'foire'* of the patron saint. (At Badefols d'Ans to St Cloud, at Le Buisson to St Firmin, at Thiviers to Ste-Croix, at Le Bugue to St Louis, at Lisle to St Roch, at Tourtoirac to St-Laurent.) At the end of the summer there will be firework displays, *'feux d'artifices'*, unsophisticated street dances, *'bals'*, *'fêtes nautiques'* on lakes or rivers, dozens of competitions, *pétanque*, boules, tennis, *pêche*, and cycle races, rugby, equestrian (*hippique*), car rallies, volley ball tournaments etc.

There are a few unusual ones. I have listed a brief selection to whet your appetites.

In **June**, Montpon-Ménéstrol has a Twirling festival (drum majorettes), Bergerac has an archery contest, Sarlat the national judo contest, Dussac a dog fair (*foire canine*), Mareuil a national riding contest, and Riberac and Périgueux have the Gascon *'vaches landaises'* and Spanish *corridas* (cow and bull fights).

In **July**, Jumilhac le Grand has its cherry fair, Sarlat a night

cycle race, Périgueux a song-fest (*concours de chant*), Le
Buisson its '*foire aux vins*', Périgueux a hang gliding contest,
St Antoine de Cumond a carnival with '*chars fleuris*' (floats
with flowers), Brantôme a major fireworks display and
operetta in the park, Bergerac regattas on the river Dordogne,
Sarrazac a '*fête du mouton*', Monpazier horse races, Vitrac a
marathon, Sigoulès a wine fair, Les Graulges donkey races,
Bergerac a beautiful baby contest and baseball tournament,
and Le Bugue a rodeo.

In **August** Lalinde has the '*fête périgorde du rugby*' (which
must be warm work), Corgnac has a '*soirée sardinades*'
(Iberian dances), Hautefort has a farming event with tastings
of '*viande limousine*', Salignac-Eyvignes a '*fête à l'ancienne,
vieux metiers*', Bourdeilles a '*défilé de chars*', Neuvic sur l'Isle
a '*Bourse aux armes*', and Brantôme a '*fête Franco-
Brittanique Alienor d'Aquitaine*'. Rouffiac has a regatta, little
St Aulaye a '*foire aux vins et aux fromages*', Belvès an aerial
display at the aerodrome called Camp de César. What of
Brantôme's '*répas périgourdin*' with '*animation avec les Gym's
Girls*'? Périgueux has a '*concours de meilleur pâté de
Périgueux*' in the Place St Louis — you need a lot of
abstinence to prepare for that! Siorac en Périgord has a '*foire
aux vins et produits regionaux*', and St Médard d'Excideuil a
'*fête de l'écrevisse*' (crayfish), Eymet a donkey race and
fireworks, and Sorges its eighteenth Dog Fair!

I suggest that on the very first day of your holiday you ask
your nearest tourist office about the events taking place within,
say, a 30 km radius, and make a note in your diary to visit
those that appeal to your family. Probably the most important
are: the Souillac jazz festival in July; the summer festival in
Gourdon; Rocamadour — *Son et lumière*, and pilgrimage
week starting 8th September; St Céré music festival mid July
— mid August; Montignac holds the Périgord festival in the
3rd week in July; Sarlat has its drama festival early August;
Périgueux its pantomime festival in August; and Gourdon its
harvest festival.

Some curiosities

Azerat on the N8 40 km east of Périgueux is built on a grid
basis. Was it meant to be a *bastide* town? But there are no

others north of the line Vergt-Domme-Bretenoux! And Saint-Aulaye 30 km west of Riberac is reputed to be a *bastide* town. But they were **only** built much further south. Mysteries!

Auriac-du-Périgord on the D67 a few km north of Montignac has a pilgrimage to the chapel of St Rémy.

La Bachellerie on the N89 38 km east of Périgueux has a honey museum.

Belvès. Saturday walnut market in late autumn.

Breuil near Beyssac on the D47 12 km east of Les Eyzies is a curious Gaulish village, a cluster of small stone cabins or *'bories'* of Neolithic times. There is another at La Salvie east of Sarlat.

Cenac. Wine festival in August.

Chancelade Abbey. Fresco depicting St Thomas à Becket.

Jumilhac-la-Grand. Château floodlit in summer with fantastic grey pepperpot towers.

Hundred Years War. Final battle monument near the D936 west of Lamothe-Montravel where General Talbot was killed.

Javerlhac northwest of Nontron has a dovecot with 1500 pigeon 'nests', and ancient forges.

Ladornac near Terrasson has an eighteenth-century water-stoup.

'Lanternes of the Dead' at Cherveix-Cubas, Atur and Sarlat are mysterious stone-built 20-30 foot cone-shaped religious buildings with four or more rectangular openings on the first 'floor'. Built in the late twelfth century.

Knights-Hospitaliers'. Best site at Condat-le-Lardin on the D62.

Salamander design. François I symbol in several streets in Périgueux.

Paper making centre. Couze-et-St Front on the D660 near Lalinde. Fifteenth-century mills and twentieth-century courses and 'stages'.

Roman wash-house at Montcaret on the D936 west of Ste-Foy-la-Grande.

Walnut Museum. Château at Doissat southeast of Belvès. Markets of Belvès and Doissat.

Tombs. King of Patagonia in Toutoirac. French Foreign Legion at Douzillac.

Film Fame (1) Eugène le Roy's book *'Jacquou le Croquant'* filmed at Fanlac west of Montignac.
(2) Chabrol's film *'Le Boucher'* made in Tremolat on the river Dordogne halfway between Bergerac and Sarlat.

Wickerwork. Fairs in Riberac on Wednesday — May/September.

Tobacco. Conducted tours *'route du tabac'* from S.I.s at Sarlat and Bergerac. Headquarters in the sixteenth-century abbey of Saint Cyprien.

Turkey. Fête at Varaignes near Nontron on 11th November.

Pottery. From old kiln south of La Roque-Gageac.

Strawberry centre. Vergt south of Périgueux has a Friday market April-November.

Truffles. Museum at Sorgès 17 km north of Périgueux (truffle hunt!)

Dolmens near Tocane-Saint-Apre west of Périgueux (Pierre-levée) and Valeuil southwest of Brantôme, called Laprouges and Coutoux.

Cheese. Trappist monks, cheese from Trappe de Bonne Esperance on the D708 southwest of Riberac.

CHAPTER SEVENTEEN: BUYING A HOUSE IN THE DORDOGNE

My wife and I were almost founder members of the Dordogne home-owning club. In 1964 I was running an advertising agency in New York and happened to see a remarkable advertisement in the airmail edition of the *Daily Telegraph*. It was beautifully written. In five lines the Arcadian charm of a two hundred year old stonebuilt farmhouse with its land, fruit trees and views was extolled. At a peppercorn price! Due for leave back in Europe, advert in hand, we drove to northern Quercy (near Cahors) where we met an English entrepreneur who, returning to Cornwall from Australia, happened to purchase a beat-up cottage in the heart of the beautiful French countryside. (It was a bit more complicated actually . . .) He soon realised that because of the gradual twentieth century exodus of youngsters from the countryside, many farmhouses, manorhouses, even châteaux, were becoming empty and unwanted. And the local estate agents had, therefore, long lists of property they could sell. As late as 1987 the leading agent in Cahors had 400 properties on his books and sold on average less than one a week.

The house buying/selling commission structure in France is inflexibly high. The current *Tarif des commissions* is as follows:

First 50,000 francs of value	8%
Next 50,000	7%
Next 50,000	6%
The band 150,000–350,000	5%
The band 350,000–700,000	4%

So on a house costing about £70,000 (say 700,000 francs) the additional cost on top of the selling price is 34,500 francs (or nearly £3,500). Therefore most local estate agents,

'*Agences Immobilières*', are happy to split their handsome commission with a British agent who can provide clients to move the dormant properties on his books.

Back to my story. Our newfound friend (who still practices in southern Quercy) provided a list of some 40 properties marked on a map, each one with a blurb of which Mr Brooks of Fulham fame would have been proud. He and his companion led the way in a dashing sports car. I saw the fourth property and fell in love with it on the spot, although my wife reminded me that we still had another 36 to see. I committed ourselves verbally and said 'I want that property.' It makes me blush to recall how little it cost us. Set in 30 acres of woods, fruit trees (cherry, plum, apple, peach, walnut), and a vineyard, was a substantial square stone house, nearly two centuries old. It had a huge attic, a courtyard with stone bakehouse and wood shed, a superb terrace overlooking a peaceful green-blue valley with hamlet, church and small river. Sheep grazing etc! Moreover a large stone built barn about 1km away in the estate grounds was included in the ridiculous price, which ten years later we sold, as our offspring for whom it was destined, preferred the city lights. The price we received for the barn, even allowing for inflation, was double that of the original value of the whole estate. Incidentally one statutory law still holds good. After a price has been agreed for a property with land over 2,500 sq. metres by buyer and seller, the *notaire* publishes the details so that a local farmer or land owner if he so wishes can match the price and buy for his own family. It is very rare indeed for this to happen, as unfortunately the majority of French small-holders and farmers are elderly and distinctly not rich!

Surprise, surprise

There were a few surprises. Surprise number one came at the purchase ceremony with the *notaire* (notary who acts for both parties, no need for solicitors and land searches) when I was about to sign the completion. The English agent reminded his naive client (me) that his commission was payable '*en plus*' by French law. It was slightly embarassing but legitimate, although he should have spelt it out in his literature. Currently

183

allow 10%–12% for extras including commission and *notaire's* fees.

Surprise number two was that the local farmer thought he had permanent grazing rights for his 200 sheep on our pasturelands. This included straight line destruction of our many drystone walls, which I had great pleasure in rebuilding to 50% above their previous height, and growing his vegetables in our fertile vineyard soil. But this was sorted out peacefully, especially since he was responsible for digging up our own truffles and rendering a very small due back to Caesar!

Surprise number three was how friendly all the locals were at this phenomenon. 'Les Anglais' had arrived (again – the first time since the Hundred Years War, when our troops apparently caused havoc in the neighbourhood).

Surprise number four was at the end of our first family summer holiday when the air around the house grew distinctly odiferous (i.e. pongy). Sherlock Holmes investigated at once and discovered that the bathroom and WC plumbing just went out into the back garden, which was therefore lush and verdant. The marvellous father and son *maçons* (stone-masons) soon built a concrete septic tank, which is still there working beautifully.

Surprise number five was the incredibly low annual land taxes payable, even with a good deal of land.

Getting sorted

Apart from new electrics to our specification and the replacing of the earth floor in the *'cave'* (ground floor where the cows used to be kept in winter) with cement to create two extra rooms, installation of a new bathroom and selection of our own apropriate furniture, the work and expenditure was negligible. No town gas of course, but bottled gas fuelled cooker and water heater. Rain water from the large roof was cycled thorugh a charcoal filter into a huge concrete tank in the *'cave'*, which, despite my wife's fears, never ran dry throughout the hottest summers. An electric pump pushed the water up to kitchen and bathroom.

It is rare to find official house surveys being carried out. Cracks in masonry on outside walls obviously should be looked at closely. The original oak beams in our house had a lot of woodworm holes (but little active). As the beams were often 20 feet long by 20 inches square we could detect easily if there might be a load-bearing problem. Always look closely at the attic timbers and roofing. We had heavy old fashioned roman-style tiles overlapping each other and tending to slip in place. The more modern red-brick rectangular tiles interlock and cannot slip.

Although our house was some distance from the nearest village we had an amiable baker who delivered three times a week. There was a weekly bus to Cahors on market day in case we did not want to use the car. Both passed the door, which was convenient. The second nearest village, within easy bicycling distance, had every shop needed including a post office, hairdresser, an excellent small hotel-restaurant (very important!). The postman (*facteur*) called every day in his little yellow van and not only delivered, but accepted mail for posting.

Our original entrepreneurial English estate agent claimed to have sold 200 properties to his compatriates in a four or five year period. I do not doubt him for a moment. In the Dordogne and the Lot there must be now several thousand English-owned properties giving their owners an enormous amount of pleasure.

Planning your purchase

Recently I have looked at estate agents windows in a dozen towns in the Dordogne and noted their name and address q.v. and even as this book is written there are many cottages available from 150,000 francs and houses from 200,000 francs. Of course you should allow an extra equivalent sum to bring the property up to scratch. Local plumbers, carpenters, electricians and masons are very reliable and in my experience carry out excellent work. But they accept more work than they can handle comfortably so if you are not on the spot to chivvy them it may not get done. Always ask for a detailed *Devis* or written estimate. It is expected and honoured and any deviation is always discussed and agreed. (Quality of wood for shutters or the height of a new terrace wall and type of stone). Keep receipted invoices for repair work. Capital gains tax (which reduces at 5% per annum. i.e. nothing payable after 22 years) can be offset by improvements carried out during ownership.

Mortgages up to 50% of the purchase price can be arranged locally at rates currently considerably less than in the UK. Mortgage services are offered for purchase of French properties by several UK companies which are shown at the end of this chapter. The French Credit Agricole bank is also helpful for local mortgages.

Some UK estate agents who specialise in French property sales, such as Barbers of Fulham (01-381-0112) produce an excellent detailed summary of everything you need to know if you are contemplating making a purchase, including cheap reconnaissance flights to the area. For instance 'Emigrating to France', 'Working Abroad', 'Local Taxes', as well as the quite simple buying ritual (*Compromis de Vente*, deposit requirements, completion, methods of payment, power of attorney etc.)

It is impossible to give advice as to where to buy and what to buy. Look at as many areas as you can. The fact that Riberac and Eymet are popular merely means that if you ever feel lonely there are other Brits around, but do look at the *bastide* countryside. My own recommendation, if you are reasonably fit, is to buy a property with as much land as you can afford, particularly with trees for privacy. We owned several thousand trees and I enjoyed thinning them. We had an excellent woodburning stove for which I must have accumulated five years log supply! My vineyard of some 400 vines gave me enormous pleasure, although it was badly neglected for many years. Spending three weeks summer holidays is not sufficient to tend vines; they need pruning in late autumn/early spring, training along wire, sulphating, quite apart from the vintaging process in the autumn.

Finally always use an English-based estate agent. It costs no extra and you get good sound advice about the area and help with pre-planning before a visit. Barbers are now selling over 100 properties a year and Miles Barber knows the Dordogne well.

Selected UK based estate agents

1. Barbers, 417–429 North End Road, London SW6 1NX, tel. 01-381-0112 (Miles Barber)
2. Property France, Portway, Wantage, Oxon OX12 9BU, tel. 0235-772211 (offer video)
3. Property 1992 Ltd, 74 Elms Crescent, London SW4, tel. 01-622-3975
4. Les Clos de France, London House, 26–40 Kensington High St, London W8 (Emily Anson)
5. Rutherfords, 197 Knightsbride (4th floor), London SW7 1RB, tel. 01-584-4392
6. Babet, 14 High St, Godalming, Surrey GU7 1DL, tel. 04868-28525 (Périgord vert)
7. Ryder International, tel. 04252-77178
8. French Affair, tel. 01-381-8519
9. D.L.P, tel. 0865-310790

French regional estate agents
(tel prefix from England 010-33)

1. Agency Klarer, 'L'Axion', Corgnac Sur Isle, 24800 Thiviers, tel. 5355 0922
2. Agence G. Boyer, 14, rue Jean Jarues, Thiviers, tel. 5355 0632 (pub. Périgord Weekly)
3. Perivert, tel. 0626 873869 (Périgord Vert)
4. Keith Wilson, 4 rue de Paris, 24260 Le Bugue, tel. 5307 2323 (Périgord Nord)
5. Immobilier 24, 24 Bvd Montagne, Bergerac 24100, tel. 5394 7566
6. Lorenzon, Le Meyrand, Cuneges, 24240 Sigoules (nr Monbazillac)
7. Immob. P. R. Giraudel, 37 Place Gambetta, Eymet.
8. Immob. Salat, 16 rue de Verdun, Nontron, tel. 5356 1634 (with English manager)
9. Immob. Chardit, rue Neuve, Bergereac, tel. 5357 2782
10. Albione Immobiliere, 2 rue Fenelon, Sarlat, tel. 5331 2872
11. Immob, Hubert Jardin, Impasse des Violette, Sarlat
12. Immob. Cadouin, tel. 5322 5608 (English spoken)

13. Immob. Albione, Allees due Republique, Gourdon
14. Hubert Jardin, 34 Ave Caraignac, Gourdon
15. Immob. Guy Vigneron, 14 rue President Wilson, Perigueux
16. Agence Lachaize, 36 rue Taillefer, Périgueux
17. L. Valora, the French Connection, Place National, Riberac (see Barbers)
18. Agence du Centre, 34 rue Gambetta, Brantome, tel. 5305 7068
19. Agence Valadie, 47210 Villereal, tel. 5336 0827
20. Immob. Montillaud, Ave Gambetta, Mussidan
21. Agence R. Chastanet, Terrasson-la-Villedieu, tel. 5350 0656

Mortgage facilities

Pleasurewood Property Sales, Anglia House. Marina, Lowestoft NR32 1HH, tel. 0502-500964

Richard Boden/David Rossiter, tel. 0272 251178 or 0272 297211 ex 3206

Charles Hamer Financial Services. tel. 01-579-8111 or 01-579-5144

Legal advice

Sean O'Connor & Co, 113 High St, Tonbridge TN9 1DL, tel. 0732-365378

INDEX